Couples' Therapy

A Do-It-Yourself Guide to a Better Relationship

Ariel S. Compton, MD

Cover Design and Illustrations: Tim Barker
www.timbarkerstudio.com
Edited by Dawn W. Petersen

ISBN: 1470056992
ISBN 13: 9781470056995

To
Richard

Table of Contents

Introduction

Your relationship is in trouble. You're scared. How can this be happening when you were so in love? There are issues that divide you. You feel you can't talk to your partner. Worst of all, you feel a sickening awareness that the person you care most about is angry with you, and, indeed, you're angry with him or her!

How do you get back together again? How do you regain your couple power, that wonderful state of feeling you have an ally, a friend, who is there just for you?

In the first glow of happiness at finding someone to love, few of us anticipate the stress of living together as a couple. We may have been prepared to promise to be together, in sickness and health, until death do us part, but few of us were prepared for the stress of everyday conflicts.

The purpose of this book is to help you regain, or perhaps find for the first time, the ability to work with, rather than against, each other. It is written for the many couples for whom therapy is not an option, in hopes of providing a way for them to work on their relationship in the privacy of their home, at little or no cost.

Each chapter begins with a discussion and then is followed by a workshop that will guide you, as a couple, through an hour just as if you were in a therapy session. All couples are unique, but the individual chapters focus on issues that are common to all relationships, such as love, money, sex, and so forth.

In the first chapter you will learn how to use this book. In the second chapter you will be guided through a workshop on communication. Read this chapter as well as chapter 1, for being able to communicate (talk to each other) is a prerequisite for the sessions that are to come. After that you can pick a chapter that is most closely related to your problem.

The chapters provide a setting in which to discuss everyday problems as well as emotionally charged conflicts that might be hard to handle on your own without a framework. They also can be used to work through more serious conflicts—and even to find a way back to each other if you have reached a point of separation or are considering divorce.

However, for some couples, emotions may be simply too strong to handle a session on their own, and they will need the help of a therapist. And certain problems, such as infidelity, or drug or alcohol abuse, or a potential for physical violence, will also need outside help. Nevertheless, even if you have doubts, give the workshops a try. You may be surprised at how well it goes.

The book is meant for all couples, married or unmarried, gay or lesbian—for the principals of love apply to all. As a matter of convenience, I have used "he" or "she" in the book, but this is not meant to designate one sex or the other. And, for a similar reason, at times I have incorrectly used a singular subject, such as "partner," with reference to a plural pronoun, such as "they, them, or their." Please forgive my deviation from the rules of grammar and adjust the reference as it may be suitable in your own individual case.

Part I

Relating To Each Other

Chapter 1

How To Use This Book

No matter how much you love each other, when you live together day after day, conflicts arise. Life itself brings problems. Partnerships are not easy.

As children, we read fairy tales that ended with "and then they lived happily ever after"; perhaps it would have served us better if they had ended with "and then the work began." For, in real life, every relationship demands work. The true test of love is the willingness to work with another to make the relationship work.

Making the Relationship Work

The first step to making a relationship work is being able to talk together; however, the last thing in the world you may want is to have to "talk about your problems." Perhaps you're being coerced into therapy by your partner's threat of leaving—"If things don't change ... ." Perhaps you are at the end of your rope and don't know where else to turn. Whatever the reason, now you are looking for help.

The purpose of this book is to provide that help, to give you a structure, a guide to use, when you have reached an impasse that is hard to get through on your own. Each chapter deals with a specific problem area and is designed to serve as a substitute for an actual hour with a therapist.

When you begin a chapter, I would like you to feel as if you have actually walked into my office. I would like you to suspend your judgment and allow yourself to be guided by the book as if I were there guiding you myself.

This is a lot to ask, I know. I won't have a chance to persuade you in person. I won't be there to intervene if things get out of hand. However, if you're willing to follow the structure of this book, it can be a guide through rough times. It can provide a way back to each other.

Setting the Stage

One or both of you may have some reluctance about beginning. This is natural. Perhaps you don't know whether or not you want to stay in the relationship. Perhaps there are things you don't want to reveal or don't want to hear.

Think about it, however. What do you have to lose? And if you have children, there is so much to gain. If you have any doubt at all, it can't hurt to try.

But don't do it halfheartedly. If you're going to give therapy a chance, give it a fair chance. Give it all you've got!

The Chapters

Each chapter of the book is divided into two parts: a discussion and a workshop. The discussion, which introduces the subject, is to provide a shared base of knowledge, a springboard, for the workshop that follows.

In the workshop, you will relate directly to each other, at times using a dialogue I have provided. Not easy, but not impossible either.

The dialogue has grown out of many years of my experience working with couples. You may feel it is not what you want to say, but if you follow it rather than branch off on your own, it can ease the tension and smooth the way. Words can be healing on their own.

You may feel foolish saying words that are not your own, but a little foolishness may not be such a bad thing. Laughter beats anger any day!

The workshops, however, will not help everyone. Perhaps you'll find one workshop that is very successful and you accomplish a great deal, but another may not work at all. A lot depends on the problem and how your personalities interact. Sometimes the problems are too deep to talk about or too intense to handle on your own. When you go for professional counseling, the therapist modifies and directs the sessions to meet your particular needs. A book can't do that.

I recommend you try a workshop. If it doesn't work, try another one or two before you give up. This need not be a wasted effort, for if the experience leads you to seek professional help, this may in itself save your relationship.

The Workshop

Beginning the workshop is a little like getting on a train. You go where it takes you. There is no getting off on your own because you suddenly think of another direction. To make the session work, you have to stay on track.

The attitude you bring is important, too. It is the baggage that sets the tone for what is to come and will make the trip a bad or good one. As you follow the steps below, try to make your tone of voice reflect a loving attitude.

STEP #1: Say To Your Partner:

"I AM LOOKING FORWARD TO OUR SESSIONS. I WILL TRY TO GIVE THEM MY VERY BEST."

This may not be the way you are actually feeling, but saying the words can help start the session off on a positive note—even if the underlying foundation is very shaky.

You may have doubts about beginning the session, but you want to do all you can to start it in the right direction. Perhaps better to say: "I am apprehensive about our sessions, but I will try to give them my very best."

STEP #2: Choose A Time For The Sessions

Set aside time for at least one, one-hour session per week. It is difficult to know in the beginning how many sessions you will need. Serious issues will warrant scheduling at least two to three more, and often it is helpful to schedule a follow-up session just to see how effective a session has been.

Make the sessions a priority. Treat each hour with the same respect you would have for a therapist's appointment—one that you are paying good money for. Don't cancel or be late.

When you put other things first, you are sending a message that your partner is not that important to you. Don't let that happen. Give your relationship a chance, keep your commitment, and come to the sessions on time.

Have a clock visible so you both can see how the time is going and when to stop. Sessions should be for one hour and not go over. Do not discuss the session or continue the discussion outside the hour.

STEP #3: Choose A Place For The Sessions

The place you choose is also important. It should be quiet, pleasant, and private. It is imperative that you take no phone calls, turn your beeper off, and don't answer the front door.

In particular, children can be a problem while you are trying to have a therapy session on your own. One couple tried to retire to the kitchen for their session while the children were entertained by television in the living room. It didn't work! The two boys started fighting with each other over which program to watch, and the little girl became quite upset when the kitchen door was shut and she could hear Mommy and Daddy talking on the other side. She began pounding on the door and crying.

Believe me, if you need to get a sitter, it is worth it!

It is also important that the place you choose is comfortable. You should be able to sit and look at each other. You should have a space on which to write or take notes. The kitchen table may serve the purpose, or perhaps it is better to get out of the house. The car, although not ideal, can at least provide privacy. If you have a park nearby, take a blanket to sit on.

I don't recommend drinking coffee and soft drinks or snacking during the session. Your attention needs to be given to each other, not to food. However, it is helpful to have a brief transition period in which to ease the return to everyday life, and some couples like to plan a brief outing after the session—an outing in which the contents of the session are put behind and left until the following session.

STEP #4: Choose A Chapter For The Next Session

What is it you want to work on? To change? Where do you think the difficulty lies? Sometimes it comes as a surprise to find that each of you sees the problem quite differently. For example, you might say the problem is "sex," whereas your partner may say "money." You might say "communication"; your partner might say "control."

Glance through the table of contents and choose the chapter most closely related to your problem. Among the topics, you will find chapters on sex, on love, on communication, on having children, and so forth. You might not be able to agree where to start, but that's all right. Pick one chapter and plan to go on to another at a later time.

STEP #5: Agree Not To Leave The Session Early Or Go Over The Time Allotted. Stop On Time.

If you become angry, upset, hurt, whatever—you still agree not to cut the hour short. Perhaps you need to leave the room for a moment to get control or calm yourself. If so, tell your partner, "Give me a moment to calm down. Please be patient. I will be right back." But to leave, to just walk out, carries a powerful and hurtful message: I can walk away from you!

So, hang in there! If your sessions are going to have a chance to succeed, you will need to control the impulse to angrily break off the session and walk out.

The one exception to this is when you truly feel you cannot control yourself. Then you need to say, "We have to stop. I don't want to lose control. We need to take a break." Hopefully, emotions won't reach this point, but if they do your partner needs to honor your request. Sometimes a breathing space, a time to reflect, is necessary.

STEP #6: Agree Not To Discuss These Sessions With Others

Confidentiality is of the greatest importance. You need to know that what you say or hear will not be repeated. The issues discussed will not be shared—not with best friends, not with siblings, and not even with your parents.

This may not be easy. There is often a great temptation to say just a few words. I remember having a very successful session in which the couple made great progress. During the hour, the man had derogatorily described himself as behaving like a "whimpering little puppy dog."

When they arrived for the next session, he looked like a thunder cloud! He sat with his arms crossed on his chest and an angry scowl on his face. For half the session he refused to say anything at all. Then suddenly he burst forth in a vituperative rage: "You betrayed me! You talked behind my back! You laughed at me!"

What had happened was that his wife had told her mother about the session. Her mother had then called him and said, "Congratulations! I hear you're not acting like a whimpering puppy dog anymore!" As you can imagine, this was indeed a setback to the therapy.

STEP #7: Ending The Hour—Shake Your Partner's Hand And Give Him/Her A Kiss On The Cheek

Say something similar to: "Thanks for participating. I'm looking forward to our next session. I love you." If you've been able to do this successfully, you are off to a good start.
CONGRATULATIONS!

Chapter 2

Communicating

"The time has come," the Walrus said,
"To talk of many things:
Of shoes—and ships—and sealing wax—
Of cabbages—and kings—
And why the sea is boiling hot—
And whether pigs have wings."

—Lewis Carroll, *Alice's Adventures in Wonderland*

Beginning a Session:

When the session begins you are both somewhat anxious, and you sit stiffly on the edge of your chairs. You have named "communication" as your main problem. "If only we could talk to each other," you say, "then we could find a way to deal with our problems."

When you first met, communicating probably wasn't that difficult. After all, you were in love. It was exciting just being together. You hadn't yet learned about the differences between you, and you hadn't built up feelings of anxiety or hurt.

How stressful it is now to hear the words, "I can't even communicate with you," or, "I can't reach you," or, "You don't understand me."

Every couple at one time or another will have trouble communicating. Sometimes women, by their nature, are more given to speech—words flow easily—whereas, for some men, it is often easier to remain silent. Words can be used to attack, but silence can be a weapon in itself.

If time has gone by, it is hard to get over the bridge of silence. It can form a wall between you. Then, when you try to open the subject again, old feelings flair up and communication is blocked. Perhaps what you want to say now is just trivia, but feelings have been so hurt in the past that you are hesitant to start. Your partner may be feeling the same.

It takes two to communicate (to convey thoughts or information to another); one person listens, while the other person talks. There is a skill to listening, just as there is a skill to talking. The person who is listening has to be receptive and attentive; the person who is talking needs to be convincing and informative but not bossy or aggressive. Communication is really a skill that can be learned. In fact, it is one of the most important skills you can have in life.

However, it is a skill you have to want to learn. If one of you doesn't want to and won't try, it is a losing battle. All I can say is, even if you feel you don't want to, why not give it a try?

You might be surprised—you might like it! What could be better than being able to talk to your partner? To understand? To share with them?

Couple Communication:

How you talk to each other, how you listen, how you convey information and thoughts, is a special part of your couple relationship. It is a way of being close, of sharing your life, your hopes and dreams, with your partner. There is an intimacy to your communication that separates it from communication with others.

In the past, communication has been primarily face-to-face, but today's technology has broadened and changed that dramatically. Cell phones, only a short time ago unknown, are now an accepted way of connecting to others. I know couples who communicate by cell phone two or three times a day, sometimes texting short messages instead.

E-mail, only a short time ago unknown, is now a quicker, easier, less expensive way of making contact than a one-to-one phone call. And the Internet has expanded our ways of communicating beyond anything we could have anticipated. Social interaction provides new ways of connecting outside of relationships. Virtual relationships (those in an electronic world rather than a real one) are becoming common.

Of course, the same skills as in face-to-face communication are important—that you present yourself in an agreeable and friendly way, that you are receptive and noncritical, that you listen attentively. But, in addition, the newer technological advances call for skills of their own, and although they offer much that is positive, there is a downside as well. Such an expansion of communication options can offer enticements that threaten a couple relationship and impinge on its borders.

An example of this is an observation I made at lunch recently. I noticed a young man and his girlfriend at an adjacent table. He was totally immersed in his cell phone call. He was in a different world. He did not speak to his companion once. When they left, he led the way, still speaking on his cell phone. She followed him—a pretty young woman who looked depressed and lonely.

I thought of recent comments by "Ask Amy"[1] in the *Los Angeles Times* when she noted that connecting emotionally to another person by cell phone could be as serious a betrayal as an actual physical relationship to another. Indeed, such betrayal of trust is not restricted to the cell phone, but can be true of other means of communication as well.

---

[1]   "Ask Amy," *Chicago Tribune* TT500, Chicago, Ill.

If this has been an issue for you, you will find a way to address it in Step #6 in the workshop.

Preparing for the Workshop

Chose a topic you would like to talk to your partner about. Make it one with some feelings involved, but not major feelings—leave those to a time when you feel more skilled at communicating.

Write down what you would like to say. Later, when you are thinking about talking with your partner, you can go over what you will say in your mind beforehand. But for this first session, put it in writing.

Keep it brief—about a paragraph. Read it aloud to yourself several times. A lot will depend on how you say the words.

Practice the inflection. Relax your face and body. Make the words gentle and friendly. Have you phrased it so there is no blame?

Words can be weapons. They can be used against another to cause hurt as well as to bring understanding. Even when not truly meant, once said, they can never be erased. They hang in the past to hurt and torment, and they can unexpectedly be used against you in the future.

It is not only the words you use, but also how they state the problem. Two suggestions can be helpful in keeping your partner receptive to what you are saying.

First, phrase what you say, if you can, so you don't cast blame. For example, instead of saying, "You are so inconsiderate. You are always late," say instead, "Do you know how upset I feel when we are late?" or "It is so hard for me when you are late. I was always taught to be on the dot!" In other words, by using "I" rather than "you," you can avoid pointing a finger.

Second, if you open with a negative phrase, you are quite likely (and understandably so) to get a negative response. Just putting something positive first can really help smooth the way.

For example, you don't like what your partner has chosen to wear. If she asks for your opinion, you could say, "That's awful! Yuck!" or you could say, "Honey, you are so pretty. That dress, in my opinion, is nice but just doesn't do you justice." This may seem contrived, but a little contriving for a good result is well worth the effort. Just a little thought can go a long way toward setting the tone.

Don't bring what you have written to the session. The most important thing you bring is the goal of wanting to share your thoughts and being willing to hear your partner's.

The Workshop

The purpose of this workshop is to provide a place where communication can be reestablished—where you can talk successfully to each other, perhaps for the first time. If you can communicate within the session, it is a skill that should carry through to all areas of your life.

STEP #1: Open By Saying, "There Is Something I Really Want To Talk To You About; Okay?"

Your partner needs to be receptive, in a listening mode. If they are not receptive, say, "That's okay. We'll schedule another time."

STEP #2: Say What It Is That You Want To Say

Don't go on too long. Do it in a friendly way. Try to have good eye contact.

STEP #3: When Finished, Ask, "What Are Your Thoughts About What I've Said?"

Resolve not to be upset as you listen if your partner differs from you. Remember, the goal is to exchange thoughts, not to be the boss presenting answers.

STEP #4: Now It Is Your Turn To Listen. Don't Interrupt. Give Your Partner A Chance To Express Their Feelings. Listen Quietly. Listen Receptively.

Remember, this is a dialogue, a conversation, not a battle or a competition to prove who is right or who is wrong. If you feel attacked, don't defend yourself. Not now! Instead, listen with the goal of understanding.

Put yourself in your partner's shoes. See if you can understand their point of view. How do they see it? Have they misunderstood you? Did they hear your words with a different meaning than you intended? Try to control your emotions and hear them out.

Even if you don't agree with them, or think they have it wrong, wait—don't interrupt. Be aware of the expression on your face. Do you look as if you are about to attack? Vomit? Or are you a loving, supportive listener trying your best to understand?

STEP #5: Ask, "Did You Understand What I Was Trying To Say? Did You Like The Way I Said It?"

If the answer is "yes," congratulations! You've taken the first step toward communicating. If the answer is "no," ask what you could have done better. Don't take affront at what they say. Listen and learn. Then say, "Thank you for listening to my thoughts. I appreciate that."

In the earlier discussion, reference was made as to how modern technology has introduced new ways of communicating into our lives. Sometimes such outside communication can diminish or encroach upon a couple's relationship. If you have such concerns, you might like to add the next step to your session.

STEP #6: Ask Your Partner: "Do You Feel Shut Out By My Use Of E-Mail, My Cell Phone, Or By Other Outside Activities?"

Listen, without feeling criticized, to your partner's feelings. If they have been feeling left out, it is important you know this.

That ends the session. In the next session your partner will be the one who chooses the topic. Your role will be to listen and "hear" (understand) what they have to say: to be successful, both a good talker and a good listener are needed.

Chapter 3

On Relating

At best, the renewal of broken relations is a nervous matter.

—Henry Brooks Adams, *The Education of Henry Adams*

When you fall in love with someone, you assume the ability to relate will follow naturally—that is, the ability to be in tune, to be empathetic and understanding—will follow naturally.

Wrong! It doesn't.

Relating to others is something you have to learn. It involves more than just transferring knowledge (communicating); it also involves a degree of emotional connection. Even more than that, however, even more than loving your partner, it involves being able to see and appreciate their point of view—even if it doesn't agree with your own!

Unless you are truly extraordinary, you weren't born knowing how to relate. Just think about it. If you were an only child, you certainly didn't have a chance to learn how to relate. You didn't need to—you were already the center of attention.

On the other hand, if you had siblings, you had to learn certain ways of being just to survive. Whether you were one of many, or even just one of two, you had to learn to compete and to struggle to get your fair share.

Many people continue to act in a couple relationship just as they did with their siblings. They are rivals with their mate. Fairness is a big issue. They want to be sure their partner doesn't get more than they do, and they are more concerned with "getting their fair share" than with the well-being of their partner.

Relating as a couple, however, is quite different from relating as siblings. As a couple, you don't want to compete with your partner. You want to be on their side. You want their happiness as much as you want your own.

Although you may know this, when your only learning experience has been with siblings, it's more than easy to fall back into old patterns of sibling rivalry. You begin to see your partner as someone struggling against you, out to win over you. Misunderstandings are rampant. Hurt accumulates and anger grows. Conflicts are left unresolved, and gradually you find you are in separate worlds. You have stopped relating!

Recently I saw a couple who live in a divided house. The husband lives upstairs, the wife down. Although they share the kitchen, they are careful to time their cooking and eating so they don't meet. If they do happen to meet it is very stressful and often leaves them upset for days.

What's happened to this couple?

Long ago they stopped relating.

Why?

It was the only way they knew to handle the pain between them. He had been unfaithful to her, not once, but many times. Each time she had grown more bitter and angrier. Each time he had grown guiltier and more distant.

With each confrontation, they had grown further apart, and with each passing day, the barriers between them grew still higher. Now, forty years later, they live in the same house but as strangers. Yet, in their own way, they still care. When she is sick, he spends hours making a special soup for her and, for a moment, when he brings it in she feels a surge of love for him; but when she is better and her strength is back, she remembers her hurt and returns the soup with the comment that "it's too salty." Didn't he know she is on a low-salt diet? Is he trying to kill her?

And so it went. Until she became so seriously depressed, she stopped eating, and he became frightened. Even then, they wouldn't have come for help on their own. It was only at their daughter's insistence that they finally came to see me.

You may wonder, in such a severe case, did therapy help?

The answer is yes.

Yes, it helped a lot, and it helped their children and their grandchildren. The repercussions of the healing between them spread like ripples in ever-widening circles, bringing a sense of hope and well-being to the entire family—because anger breeds anger and more anger, but love breeds love and more love.

This is an extreme example, but over the years I have seen many couples who were so filled with hurt and anger that they lived in separate worlds. The house they lived in might as well have been divided, and they were like strangers speaking different languages.

If this has happened to you, how do you begin to relate again? How do you take the first step?

THE FIRST STEP IS YOUR WILLINGNESS TO TAKE YOUR PARTNER BACK INTO YOUR LIFE.

The first step is a mental step—one you take entirely on your own. No one can make you take it. You can only take it when you want to, when you see the sense to it, when you are ready to.

If you are like many people I have seen, you have a tremendous amount of resistance to this step. You probably want your partner to be the one to take the first step, not you.

"You be willing to take me back first!"

"You be willing to stop arguing first!"

"You tell me you're sorry first!"

Such unwillingness to take the first step is often a mark of pride. I remember as a child I had a book with a picture about pride. When the book was open, the picture covered two pages. On the left it showed a little man walking along with his nose up in the air. On the right it showed a terrible cliff. Under the picture it said, "Pride goes before a fall!"

And so it does! Pride serves no purpose, but keeps the barriers up. If you can see how foolish it is to let pride keep you from relating to the person you love, you will be able to give it up.

Another form of resistance is the thought: It's too late! It has gone on too long!

As long as you are alive, it's never too late! But time does eventually run out, and time spent in anger is wasted time.

Or you might think, But I can't stand being rejected again.

So?

Everyone gets rejected. A thousand times. So you're rejected—so what! It doesn't have to be such a big deal. You can reduce the hurt and dull the pain somewhat by being prepared—that is, by knowing a rejection may come and saying to yourself mentally, "It's okay. I can take it. I'll survive." And, truly, isn't the chance to be able to relate again worth the chance of being rejected?

THE SECOND STEP IS TO LEARN HOW TO CONVEY WHAT YOU ARE TRYING TO SAY THROUGH YOUR BODY LANGUAGE AS WELL AS THROUGH THE WORDS YOU USE.

As mentioned in the previous chapter on communication, how you say something can be as important as what you say. The second step, or perhaps it would be better to say a companion step, is a physical one.

Now that you have decided that you want to relate again, you have to show it in the way you act: in the way you look at your partner, the way you hold yourself, how you move. You show it in your tone of voice and the words you choose. When you add "relating" to communication, you add a new and different dimension of empathy and understanding.

Do you realize how much the meaning of the word you say is determined by how you say it?

Let me give you an example. The word "right" is a great word to practice on. Try it. You can make it a bullet of hatred. A friendly affirmation. A denial. A put-down. A rebuff. You can make it whatever you wish, merely by the inflection you give it.

Do you realize how important the way you physically approach your partner is?

Are you crouched, like a beast about to leap? Are you "in" your partner's face, hostilely and aggressively invading their space? Or are you distant, a million miles away in the corner of the bedroom?

Are you within touching distance?

Touch, when it conveys anger, does great harm, but touch can carry love as well. It's amazing what touch at the right moment can do. It's a form of communication in itself. It can be a caress like the flutter of a butterfly. It can be a message saying, without words, "I'm sorry." Or a plea: "Please accept me again."

If you are willing to take your partner back into your life, and if you are willing to use your body to convey that message, you are ready to begin the workshop.

The Workshop

STEP #1: Please Say To Your Partner:

"I WANT TO TRY AGAIN. I WANT TO RELATE TO YOU. PLEASE GIVE ME A CHANCE. I WILL DO THE BEST I CAN."

This step is not an easy one. The first step never is.

Often feelings get in the way of relating. You are probably both feeling angry, possibly hurt, so it is very hard to put those feelings aside and act as if everything is okay. Nevertheless, that is what I am going to ask you to try to do.

You may be thinking, but that isn't how I really feel. Isn't it dishonest to act in a way I don't feel?

No.

Feelings are emotions that sometimes have little to do with reality. Their roots can be in the past, not the present. The false belief that it is always good to let out feelings has unfortunately led to many a breakup.

No. It is not dishonest to contain painful or angry feelings in order to begin relating again. But how, when you are under the power of a wave of anger, do you do this?

STEP #2: Containing Anger

Anger in itself is not bad. In fact, it is necessary. It tells us when we are being stepped on, when something needs to change. Usually the source of anger is hurt. The purpose of anger then should be to change the situation that is causing our pain, not to lash out at the person we love.

31

Anger, when it is too intense, destroys our ability to relate. Men in particular are very sensitive to anger in a woman, perhaps because it reminds them of an angry mother. Women are sensitive to anger also. For many women, anger reinforces a terrifying fear of being unloved.

Knowing this, can you put your anger on hold? Can you say to your partner, "It is true I'm angry with you, but I will try to direct my anger at the problem and not at you"?

In addition to keeping a rein on anger, what else is necessary to be able to relate? The next step is very straightforward, but not at all easy to do. However, a simple example, which you've probably heard before, can be helpful in visualizing what you need to do.

Some time ago when my husband and I visited the Galapagos Islands, we were told the wildlife had never seen humans before so it was not fearful. In keeping with this, sometimes a sparrow would alight on my palm. Our leader explained to me: If you want to keep the sparrow there, continue to hold your palm open. If you try to close your fingers, the sparrow will dart away.

So it is in relating: hold the palm of your hand open and let your partner sit there freely, for if you try to grab hold, your partner will have to fight to be free. By relinquishing control, you have removed the need for a struggle.

STEP #3: Giving Up Control, Or Accepting That Your Partner Has The Right To Be Who They Are

You cannot change another person. You cannot control another person. You can only change and control yourself. One of the basics of a good relationship is that you release each other to be who you are. In this "good" relationship, you have found the one place in the world where you can be free to be yourself. Wonderful!

"Fine," you say, "but what if I really don't like who my partner is?" Or, as is perhaps more usually the case, "I like some things about them very much, but some things not at all." What then?

Well, you have several choices:

1) You can fight to change them. You can be angry and critical. You can storm and cry. Usually this doesn't work—at least not for long.

2) If the differences between you are too great, you can leave.

3) If you care too much to leave, or if leaving is impossible, you can stay and try to work it out. But how? Not by trying to control your partner and forcing them to change, but by letting them know what you want and leaving it up to them to make their own decisions.

Let's take an example of a couple in which one partner smokes and the other does not. The man is irritated, angered, and worried by the woman's continued need to smoke. She has lied in an effort to avoid his attack. She promises to quit but doesn't.

The first thing he has to realize is that he cannot change her. She is the only one who can stop smoking. There is no way he can force her.

What can he do?

He can tell her something along the lines of the following, without blame or a long lecture or an accusation of how untruthful she has been: "I am deeply troubled by your smoking. I love you very much. I want to do all I can to help you stop." If the problem is threatening the relationship, he needs to let her know how serious it is. He can add, "If your smoking continues, you need to know that it is a serious problem for me that is affecting our relationship." If the problem still continues, he may have to say, "I love you, but this is not a situation I can live with indefinitely. You need to know that."

Then she has to be as free in making her own decision as he was free to express himself. If he decides to stay and try to help her, he must accept the responsibility for staying and not blame her. If he is to continue to relate to her, he has to accept her as she is: a smoker. Then there is a chance they can work out the problem together.

If you understand what I have said and how important it is to be accepted as you are (problems and all), and how important it is to a relationship to feel you are accepted within it, you will be able to say to your partner and mean it:

STEP #4: "I Will Try To Accept You As You Are."

Having each stated your willingness to try to relate again, to put aside your anger and to accept your partner as they are, please take turns and ask each other:

STEP #5: *"What Must I Do To Relate To You Again?"*

If you are the person asking the question, your task is to listen. Listening is not easy, but it is something you can learn to do. Listening is not complex, either, but when you are sitting on a powder keg of emotions ready to explode, it takes tremendous self-control.

First, even if you don't feel it, try to look it: FRIENDLY.

Try to remove the scowl from your face, the frown from your forehead, the angry glare in your eyes. Let go of the tension your body may be feeling.

If that is too much to ask and you can't look friendly yet, what you can do is not interrupt. What you can do is not argue. What you can do is not correct. If you really can't keep from doing all these things, go to the medicine cabinet and get a Band-Aid and put it over your mouth. Then, if you can focus on what your partner is saying, not on yourself and what you are going to say, you will not only be listening, you will be relating!

When it is your turn to answer the question, "WHAT CAN I DO TO RELATE TO YOU AGAIN?" don't seize on this as an opportunity to tell your partner everything they have done wrong, or how they have failed to relate to you in the past. Instead, let them know, briefly, how they can open the door to you again.

For example, you might say, "Try not to be so angry with me; I really didn't mean to hurt you," or, "Try not to be so critical of me. I know I made a mistake, but I am trying as hard as I can," or, "Please, I know we've had problems in the past, but I can't change that now. If we could just begin with the present ... ."

As you speak, be aware of your tone of voice. Is it demanding, angry, apologetic, begging? Try to control the inflection you give your words. Look at your partner and make the expression in your eyes warm, not cold. Did you know you can consciously control this? Try it, if you have any doubt. You can make your eyes melt with affection or turn cold as ice. Your eyes, "the windows of your soul," will tell your partner if you are sincere.

When you do respond, your choice of words and how you say them will be very important. You may be tempted to say, "Well, if you would just do this or that, then I could do what you ask."

Don't. Instead, say: "I will think about what you have said. I will try to understand it. I will try to see your side. Let me think about it and I will get back to you."

Your being willing to think about it, and not retaliate with anger, is perhaps the most important part of the workshop. It means you have put aside your need to explain or defend yourself, and are really willing to consider what your partner said and to think about how to respond. You will have opened the door to relating again!

Chapter 4

Couples And Compromise

To marry is to halve your rights and double your duties.

—Arthur Schopenhauer, *The World As Will and Idea*

The basis of a good relationship depends upon your skill in being able to compromise. Two people can be deeply, intensely, passionately in love and yet not be able to live together. For living together demands the capacity and will to compromise—not just once, or now and then, but continuously in a thousand little ways, all day long.

At night in bed, do you want one blanket, two blankets, or none? Is this a good time for sex or not?

If it is time to eat, are you both hungry? Do you want to eat the same thing? What movie do you want to see? On and on, when you live with another person, both trivial and major life events demand continual compromise.

If all is going well, the process of adjusting is so easy it almost goes unnoticed. On the contrary, if it is not going well, every moment, every trivial issue has the potential to become a major conflict.

The Meaning of Compromise

Compromise can mean different things to different people.

What is compromise?

Perhaps you think compromise means having to give in. Or, on the contrary, perhaps you think it means your partner should have to give in.

Not so.

Compromise is a process whereby each of you gives a little, in turn, until a mutually satisfactory agreement is reached. For each act of giving, something must be given in return. It is like balancing a seesaw.

The further apart you are, the more difficult it will be to reach a compromise. For example, you may have little difficulty resolving which movie you want to see, but it is a decision of another magnitude to decide where you want to live, or whether or not you want to have children. In some cases, keeping the relationship may demand major sacrifices for both partners.

Sometimes Compromise Can Bring Rewards of Its Own

Mary and Tom had come to see me because of conflicts over money, but then, during one of the sessions, issues came up in regard to their vacations. Tom was a surfer who loved the ocean. He really didn't like the desert at all. Mary, on the other hand, loved the desert but couldn't care less about the ocean. This difference caused constant bickering. Neither wanted to go on a vacation separately; after all, the fun of vacationing was really the pleasure of being together.

What to do?

"Why not compromise," I asked. "One time try the desert; the next time, the ocean?"

They were reluctant—particularly Tom, who said, "I hate the desert; too hot!" Nevertheless, they agreed to compromise. Tom would try to put up with the desert if Mary would accompany him to Hawaii and watch him surf.

Following the end of their sessions, I didn't see them for several months, until I happened to run into Mary in the grocery store.

Guess what?

They had followed through on the compromise. They had gone to Palm Springs for the desert vacation, and Tom had had a wonderful time at the music festival. And Mary had loved Hawaii, even though she didn't want to go in the water, just sit on the beach and watch Tom surf. Compromise had not only improved their relationship but had enriched their lives.

And then there is the story of Francis and Scott, whose compromises were more difficult to make but that made a big difference in their relationship.

Frances and Scott had been married about ten years. They had had a good marriage, but bickering between them had increased to a point where they were feeling chronically angry with each other.

Frances was somewhat overweight—twenty pounds—and Scott would make an occasional comment such as, "I see the cookies disappeared," or, "I thought we were going to skip dessert." Comments Frances didn't respond to but that stayed with her and were upsetting. Yes, she had eaten the cookies, and yes, she had meant to skip dessert, but no, she didn't need to be reminded of this.

And then Scott, who had been a fairly heavy drinker for years, had increased his cocktails from two martinis before dinner to three. Frances would say each time, "Do you really need that third drink?" and he would say nothing but would go ahead and have the drink anyway. Then they both would feel irritated.

When these interactions and the bad feelings associated with them came out in the session, both Frances and Scott wanted to change them. They agreed to try to reach a compromise. Francis would talk to her physician about her weight and begin exercising, and Scott would save the third drink for special occasions.

An important part of their agreement was that they would be responsible only for their part of the compromise—they would not criticize each other for failing to carry out their part. They would be as supportive as possible.

This was not easy for either one of them. Despite good intentions over the next few months, they each had relapses. Frances still occasionally ate cookies or dessert when she shouldn't have, and Scott still occasionally had that third drink when he shouldn't have. However, Frances had seen her doctor and begun exercising, and Scott had taken seriously her request to keep the cocktails at two rather than three. They were quite supportive of each other, praising each other when they were successful and remaining quiet when they were not. When I saw them a year later, Frances had lost ten pounds, and Scott had (for the most part) kept the cocktails at two.

Frances and Scott were lucky. Although compromise is always worth a try, certain problems, such as weight and addictions, are difficult to handle on one's own and can require outside help.

Sometimes a compromise is asking too much. If you feel you cannot go that far, you have to say to your partner, "I'm sorry, I can't do that. You are asking more than I can give."

For example, if one of you lives in Alaska and the other in Florida, and neither one of you is willing to move, your differences are too great. A compromise is not possible, and you will have to say to each other, "We love each other, but we cannot live together."

Sometimes one partner will make immense sacrifices to adjust to the other, but this may well lead to grief. A compromise needs to be mutually satisfactory, otherwise the decision rankles beneath the surface until it finally comes to a head.

Staying with another for years while swallowing one's own wishes may be an unwise decision. Painful as it may be, it is far better to be open and honest as to one's feelings. Putting the cards on the table, where they can be talked about and worked with, is far better than the seemingly easier "going along with it" and having the hope things will eventually change on their own.

The Workshop

You have chosen this chapter because you would like to use compromise as an aid in resolving conflicts. Since the skills of communicating and relating are so important in regard to reaching a successful compromise, it is recommended you review chapters 2 and 3 before starting the workshop.

In the workshop you will be directed to answer specific questions, or you will actually be given words to say. Try to make your answers as honest and simple and direct as you can. The tone of voice, the way you say things, the expression on your face are as important as the words themselves. Set anger and hurt aside, if you can.

Try not to blame the other person. Try to present the conflict as the problem, not your partner. As pointed out previously in Chapter 2, one aid in helping you do this is how you frame what you say. Instead of saying, "You did this or that!" try using "I" instead. Say, "I felt this way or that way." Using "I" instead of "you" (which points the finger) is much easier for your partner to hear. Try it out yourself and you will see this is true.

Of equal importance as what you say, or how you say it, is how you listen when it is your turn. Listening conveys respect for the other person. Listening demonstrates a willingness to hear their side, and in return makes it much more likely that they will listen to your side. Good listening carries a message to the other person that is very powerful.

Begin the workshop with a fairly minor conflict. If you are successful in communicating and reaching a compromise, you can then move on to work with more major conflicts.

STEP #1: Say To Your Partner, "I Want To Try To Work To Reach A Compromise. Out Of Love For You, And A Wish To Make You Happy, I Will Do All I Can To Meet You Halfway."

Your attitude is critical, and a necessary part of this is that you recognize that your partner has a right to be different from you.

STEP #2: Say To Your Partner, "I Accept You The Way You Are. I Will Not Judge Or Criticize You For Being As You Are. I Will Respect You And The Differences Between Us."

Now the way is prepared for you to present your side of the conflict.

STEP #3: The Conflict

In presenting the conflict, modulate your voice so that your tone is friendly. Try to present just the facts without embellishing with feelings of hurt or anger.

At the same time, try not to be fearful and timid. If you have a tendency to be a martyr and sacrifice yourself for the other person—DON'T.

Give yourself the right to be a full person. Your partner will respect and love you more for it, not less. Denying yourself the right to assert yourself appropriately will fester inside like poison. Your not being honest, or brave enough to actually state your wishes, will, in the end, defeat your relationship.

STEP #4: Explain Why Your Position Is Important To You, What It Means To You, And Why You Feel As You Do.

Then ask, "How important is this problem for you?" and let them have their turn. Sometimes just understanding in itself can take away feelings of unfairness and create feelings of empathy. When misunderstandings are removed, you may find that the differences have been resolved on their own.

STEP #5: Actual Compromising

Ask your partner: "How much can you give up?"

Remember, since you have to live with your partner, it is important that they be as happy with the compromise as you are.

Then, after listening carefully to their response, you might ask, "What can I give you in return?" or perhaps, "Can we meet halfway?"

Remember, the goal is not to change your partner so that they are like you.

Remember, the goal is not to win. Why would you want to win over your partner?

Remember, the goal is not to prove yourself right. Why would you want to put your partner (whom you really love so much!) in the position of being wrong?

After all, aren't you a team? And on your team you want everyone to be a winner and everyone to be right. The goal is really to be on the same side. When the compromise is reached, you want your partner to be as happy with the outcome as you are.

STEP #6: Closing The Hour

Document the major points made in the session. Schedule a follow-up meeting. You may not have been able to reach an agreement, so allow time between the meetings to think about the compromise reached or to come up with alternative suggestions.

Conflict resolution is never easy. If you have made progress, congratulate yourselves! If not, say, "Next time" and leave with a kiss!

Chapter 5

Couples And Love

O, my Luve's like a red, red rose ...

—Robert Burns, *The Scots Musical Museum*

For many of us, love is the most important ingredient in our lives. Money, intelligence, beauty, accomplishments, even our health, are secondary to love. Though we may possess all the riches of the world, if we don't have love, we feel we have nothing.

In my years as a therapist, and in my life as a woman, I have learned many things about love. Now I would like to share a few of them with you.

What Is Love?

Of course, we all know what love is. Defining it, however, is a different matter.

There are many different kinds of love and many different ways of regarding love. Here, our focus is on a couple's love, and if we turn to Webster's Dictionary[2] we'll find definitions that seem to fit: "deep and tender feelings of attachment or devotion to a person or persons" and/or "a strong, usually passionate, affection for one person or another, based in part on sexual attraction."

These are as good definitions as any, but we can add a psychoanalytic one as well: Love is a flow of positive psychic energy toward an object.

To conceptualize love in this way, as a stream of energy, takes it out of the world of fantasy and gives us, individually, a little more control.

One of the most important things I have learned is that love is not just a "gift from the gods" but something we ourselves can work to create and to keep.

Although we cannot force love to come, there are certain things we can do that will make it more likely to happen. Of course, each person is different. Each couple is different. And each problem is different. Love, and the capacity to feel and give love, are extremely complex. Books and books have been written on these subjects.

So what, specifically, can this chapter on love offer you?

---

2   *Webster's New World Dictionary, Second College Edition, 1968*

It can be a starting place, a first step in looking at love a little differently and seeing that you have more control than you thought. Fairy tales we have read, the movies we have seen, the culture we live in all have contributed to misconceptions about love. Clearing away some of these misconceptions can put you on more solid ground as you work to bring and keep love in your life.

In the following section I discuss love and its relationship to sex as well as "falling in love" and its relationship to "real" love. Then, since love is a feeling we are often hesitant to express, I encourage you to be more openly affectionate to each other. Even small changes can make a big difference. A little love can go a long way!

Love and Sex

Love and sex are not the same. Although the two may be mingled together, they are very different. Love is of the mind and spirit. Sex is of the body and instincts. Love is a flow of affection that is directed towards another person. Sex is a drive, fueled by hormones, that seeks release and gratification.

Such distinctions are important because confusion between the two leads to many misunderstandings and much unhappiness. Such confusion gets played out every day in our culture, not only in the movies we see and the novels we read, but also in our own lives. Even the language we use fosters such confusion. For example, included among the definitions of love listed in

Webster's Dictionary[3] can be found both "sexual passion" and "sexual intercourse." No wonder we have a problem making a distinction in our own lives.

Let me give you a few examples of what this confusion can lead to.

One: A woman learns her husband has had sex with another woman. She assumes this means he doesn't love her. (Although it might mean this, on the other hand, it might not.)

Two: During sex, a man fails to achieve an erection. He assumes his wife will stop loving him because of this. (She may be upset over this, but her love is not based on his having an erection.)

Three: A woman walks into the bedroom and surprises her husband, who is masturbating. She leaps to the conclusion that he doesn't love her. (This may or may not be true, but masturbation is a release of sexual tension that has nothing to do with love.)

On and on. There are many examples. Perhaps you can think of several yourself.

Generally speaking, men know better than women that sex is not the same as love. For even though women are on a more equal footing with men sexually, many women, even today, cannot be casual about sex and often feel downgraded if there is no emotional involvement.

Such a difference between the way men and women view the relationship between sex and love is understandable given their different biological roles. Men's

---

3   *Webster's New World Dictionary, Second College Edition, 1968*

biological role is to maintain the human species by spreading sperm as widely as possible. Women's biological role is to have sex with the best man she can (in other words, the one she feels "love" for), and thus her selection will strengthen, not weaken, the future race. She is the recipient of the sperm. She will be the mother, the one who will bear the child and form "the family," the unit so important for raising the child. She brings tenderness and caring; in other words, she brings "love" into the relationship.

Although sex and love are both a part of a couple's life, love includes a concern for the whole person that goes far beyond having sex. It includes wanting to care for them, wanting to spend time with them, wanting them to be happy. It also includes wanting to be loved in return. A loving relationship can provide a refuge from the trials and pains of a competitive and dangerous world.

On the other hand, people have good sex all the time who are not in love with each other. Having sex with a person does not mean you love them, nor does love depend on sexual performance. Indeed, good sex is a skill that can be learned (perhaps one could compare it to a skill in cooking; one can make a good meal if one is a novice, but one can make an even better meal if he or she is an experienced chef). Love, in contrast, is not a "skill" that can be learned but springs from the heart.

Ideally, the presence of love makes sex better, but not always. Love can complicate sex by bringing in concerns of its own, such as inner prohibitions, performance anxiety, or fears of not being able to live up to the other's expectations.

Beyond Biology

Couple relationships entail far more than biology. They transcend simple gender stereotypes to encompass a broad range of committed and loving relationships.

Today, there are couples of many different kinds: married couples; unmarried couples; same-sex couples; couples who choose to have children; couples who choose not to have children; couples who were previously unable to have children and now, due to advances in fertility treatments, are able to have a family; and many other types of couples.

Despite these differences, the fundamental principles of couples' relationships remain the same: being able to communicate, to relate, to compromise, to manage money, to love, and to have sex. And among the factors that bring couples together, "falling-in-love" remains one of the most common.

Falling in Love

Just as love and sex are different entities, so "falling in love" is different from "real" love.

Certainly, falling in love is among one of the most wonderful things that can happen to us. Although it may be hard to put the feeling of "falling in love" into words, we all know what it means when someone says, "I have fallen in love with you," or, "I'm sorry, I'm not in love with you anymore."

We know such love is extraordinarily powerful. We know it is out of our control. We are as helpless to escape it as we are powerless to create it. We know it takes precedence over all other things in our lives. We are obsessed. We do not, cannot, listen to reason. It is indeed like a little psychosis. There is an old adage that one cannot do therapy with someone who is in love—for nothing can alter this state and bring them to their senses.

In psychiatry, this falling in love is often explained as a "transference reaction." There are many different definitions of a transference reaction, but perhaps it would suffice to say that it is an intense emotion that has its roots in the past but is now powerfully reexperienced in the present. Let me give you an example.

You walk into a room. Across the room you see a woman standing with sun lighting her hair. Her hair is golden and cascades down her back. She is slender, and her back is toward you. She turns, catches your eye, and smiles at you.

It happens! Your heart races and comes alive with excitement; you have the crazy thought, This is the woman I'm going to marry. You have "fallen in love" although you have never spoken with her, have yet to even meet her.

You don't know that when you were a child your mother often stood by the window in the morning playing her violin, and that the sunlight would come in and light her golden hair. At times, she would turn and look at you, and you would feel the warmth of her affection as she caught your eye. When the woman across the room turns and catches your eye, in your unconscious, the powerful effect experienced as a child in the warmth of your mother's love is reawakened and rechanneled. You fall in love!

For each of us, there are complex, individual reasons for transference reactions, but the process is always fueled from the unconscious, and when falling in love is involved, it always includes idealization in some way. This, sadly, often sets the stage for failure in the relationship, for disappointment is inevitable, sometimes even a feeling of betrayal: You are not who I thought you were!

In addition, often the idealization that accompanies falling in love is not felt equally by both partners. Therefore, one person "loves" more than the other, and this imbalance can undermine the relationship. When one partner cares more than the other, or feels less than the other, trouble lies ahead.

Thus, falling in love can be a two-edged sword, on the one hand pulling a couple together, on the other hand setting a couple up for problems ahead. There was a time when I thought falling in love was the only path to "true love." It was not until I was on a medical trip with other doctors that I learned that falling in love, as wonderful as it might seem, was not only unnecessary but was not "true" love at all.

This trip had entailed long hours traveling. During part of the trip, we gave medical lectures on our specialty, but one day when the hours were particularly long, we turned to sharing stories about ourselves.

There were thirty of us on the trip, fifteen married couples. We shared how we had met. How our lives had been. We were an older group. Of the group, half of the couples were of East Indian heritage, a different culture than mine. Their marriages had been arranged for them by their parents; falling in love had not been a factor. They had not even met prior to their marriages, yet now they all expressed gratitude to their parents and love for their partners.

None of them had ever been divorced. In their relationships, love had not been there from the start but had come gradually as a result of the interaction between them. They had caused it, fostered it, created it.

In contrast, the rest of the couples, myself included, who had described falling in love as what had led to marriage, had all been divorced. The first marriage had not worked out.

Indeed, it would seem that those who begin marriage without the magical state of falling in love are really better off. They start with both feet on the ground and want to work toward the goal of coming to love each other.

In actuality, the two types of love are quite different. Falling in love has its roots in the unconscious, whereas "real" love (although it may also have roots in the unconscious) is the result of real interaction with a real person in a real world.

Sometimes sex, or a subsequent pregnancy, may be the propelling force into a marriage, but then, as is the case with falling in love, to have real love emerge takes time and a concerted effort by each partner. Falling in love can grow into real love, but it does not happen automatically. It takes effort from both partners.

Real Love

"Real" love grows as one comes to know a person. Are they kind to you, loving to you; do they care about you? Do you like being with them? Does their way of thinking appeal to you? Do you miss them when they are gone?

Do you like their sense of humor? Sharing a joke with someone is a little like loving them. You are so close for that moment; you laugh together and that often feels like the beginning of love.

Do you like to hold them and touch them? Do they smell good so you want to nuzzle them and bury your head in their clothes? All these things are real, part of the world today, not an illusory wish projected from the past onto the present.

Perhaps most of all, real love grows as a result of reciprocal interactions between two people who come to value and appreciate each other. Although we cannot force love to come, there are certain things we can do every day that will help to nurture it and keep it alive when it is here. We forget, or we are too busy, or we are caught up in something else, and without our realizing it, love can slip away.

Keeping Love Alive

Love is fragile. It demands a lot of effort and attention.

Can love die?

Of course it can. It needs fuel, just as hunger needs food and thirst needs water. It takes work and effort every day.

One of the first and most obvious things we can do is express the love we feel inside. Be more verbal!

"I love you." No words are more welcome.

Saying aloud "I love you" to your partner creates a wonderful, healing bond. It is surprising how much power these words can have. They make the anger go out of an argument. They take the hurt away after a misunderstanding.

"I love you," however, should not be overused, or used when insincere. It will lose its power. Don't be afraid to use it every day, though. It is very comforting to have my husband say, before he falls asleep each night, "I love you." It never seems insincere to me. I never get tired of hearing him say it. Try it.

But not only the words are important. The way you say them, the tone of voice you use, are also important. You can put tenderness into the words you use.

You can be more affectionate. Reach out now and then and lovingly (not sexually, but lovingly) touch your partner. I heard once that if you want a man to become yours, the first step is to reach out and touch him. It is true. Touching has great power.

Of course, there are no guarantees. Giving love does not mean it will be returned. Life carries no promises.

In the workshop that follows, you will have a chance to talk about love, find out what it is your partner needs, and let your own need for love be known as well.

The Workshop

Discussions of love go on for a lifetime. Working on love goes on for a lifetime. The purpose of this workshop is to provide an opening for love to begin, or an opportunity to bring love back if it has been lost.

STEP #1: Setting The Stage

Recall the circumstances of your meeting. Were you in love, or were there other factors in your decision to become partners in life?

How did you meet?

Was it nice?

Are you glad you met?

Each of you take a turn reminiscing.

STEP #2: Where Are You Now?

Discuss whether love was there to begin with. Has it grown? Or has love become lost along the way?

STEP #3: Ask Your Partner, "Do You Feel You Get Enough Love And Enough Attention From Me?" (Note: not sex, but love!)

Talk about love's fragility, how life events and everyday stresses can wear on love, and how you want to give as well as receive love.

STEP #4: Ask Your Partner, "How And When Would You Like Me To Be More Loving?"

Again, this does not mean having sex; it means being more loving—tender, thoughtful, concerned.

STEP #5: Take Turns Telling About What Love Has Been Like For You

Were you loved as a child? Have you had heartbreak in life? How important is being loved to you? How do you want to be loved now?

STEP #6: Ending The Session

Say to your partner, "I want to care for you. I want you to care for me. I love you."

Did you feel you learned something about perceiving and expressing love? Did you feel loved during the workshop? If so, it was a success. If not, you have work to do.

Schedule the next session with each of you having the goal of making your partner feel more loved. Remember, this takes work and time and effort.

But it is worth it.

Every bit!

Chapter 6

You And Your Money
OR
The Money Balance

Of all the icy blasts that blow on love, a
request for money is the most chilling and
havoc-wreaking.

—Gustave Flaubert, *Madame Bovary*

Money is important! No surprise to some of you,
but what a shock to those who thought love would
sweep away such petty concerns! Such shock has
repercussions in the best of relationships and often

continues for years to send unpleasant waves through relationships.

Did you know that in much of the world today, marriages are still arranged by families? Money is very much a part of this arrangement. It may seem surprising to you that such marriages are often successful, but one contributing factor is that the rules as to money are more clearly defined.

In this country (the United States), there aren't rules to go by. It's generally left up to you, as a couple, to plow your way through the unknown pitfalls of economic togetherness. Some couples may handle it more easily than others, but for all couples it can be a challenge. The purpose of this chapter is to make it as easy as possible.

Money and You

Love can survive even a catastrophic loss of money. What it sometimes can't survive are everyday hassles over money.

"Why didn't you tell me you wrote that check?"

"I thought we were going to save something this month!"

"Do you really need that new dress?"

"Why do the kids have to go to private schools? I never did!"

Such struggles can tear a relationship apart. They can grind away until little love is left.

Lack of money could put a crimp in any relationship, but even with ample funds, the day-to-day problems of dealing with finances can make love fly out the door. The reason for this is that money is not "just money." The way you handle it says a lot about the way you relate not only to your partner but to others as well. The way you handle money tells a lot about you.

Money reveals a part of ourselves we keep hidden even from ourselves. It's not a part easily looked at, and if we are really honest about it, we might be quite shocked at what we find. Let me ask you:

How much does money really mean to you? How much do material things really matter? How much is your self-esteem tied to your bank account? How greedy are you? Do you have pangs of jealousy when you see that a neighbor has more than you? How easy is it for you to part with your money?

Money can really put your secret self to the test. Money can and does often put love to the test.

Money Puts Love to the Test

"Do you love me or my money?"

"If I lost all my money, would you still love me?"

"If I wanted money, would you give it to me, no questions asked?"

"Have you thought to provide for me if something should happen to you?"

"Am I in your will? To what degree?"

"Can I really trust you financially?"

"Do you really trust me?"

At some point in your relationship, such questions must have come to mind. However, these are risky questions and are hard to put into words. They can call love into question.

So, what do you need to do? You need to be able to talk to your partner openly. You need not to be afraid to talk about money. You need to take the shame out of talking about it. Of course you are interested in money! Everyone is! Your partner is as well, and should be. Money and its management is part of being a couple.

Your Money Style

In the past, gender was thought to have something to do with one's money style. Freud might not be in fashion today, but long ago he observed that the anal-compulsive stage of the two-year-old boy was much more powerful than that of the two-year-old girl. Thus men (little boys grown up), by their very nature, might hang on more tightly both to their emotions and to their money, while women (little girls grown up) would let emotions and money flow more easily. Indeed, observation would tend to support the fact that grown women love to shop. Perhaps it is part of "feathering the nest," for it seems to comes naturally to almost all of us.

However, this is a new world, and in this new world the roles of women and men are changing. Women are no longer relegated to the role of "housewife" but are working outside the home and often earning as much as men. And many men, some of whom once looked down on household duties, are participating more in household and parenting tasks. Indeed, perhaps differences in money style have as much to do with individual differences as they do with gender.

The question is, if you have a different money style than your partner (say one of you is a free-spender, and the other a tightwad), how do you get along at all?

The key to getting along is to make the differences between you work for you rather than against you. After all, the differences could be a good thing. If you're both savers you might forgo a lot of pleasure, and if you're both spenders you might end up in bankruptcy. However, if one of you tends to be a spender and one a saver, there's a good chance you can reach a happy medium. It just takes being able to work together.

Money Versus Love

Although you may each have a different style in regard to money, this doesn't mean you don't love each other or that one of you is more "right" than the other. Nor does it mean that it isn't possible to work out a plan with which you both can live.

Each couple is different, and your plan will need to fit your own unique circumstances; however, in general, I think it is important to allow each person to have as much financial freedom and independence as possible. The following is a plan I have found helpful.

When both partners are working and bringing in a salary, each month they contribute an agreed-upon amount to a shared domestic account, which includes all shared expenses, as well as to a joint savings account. Anything over and above the joint contributions are each partner's to put into an individual account or to spend as they so choose.

If only one partner is working and bringing in the income, and the other is carrying the responsibility for the household, then the earned income should be shared. An agreed-upon portion should go to the "stay-at-home" partner to be put in their individual account. Such a plan gives equal recognition to the "stay-at-home" partner, something that is long overdue.

Setting up such a plan is easier done at the beginning of a relationship, but it's never too late. Indeed, the following workshop is a good place to begin.

The Workshop

As it is for all the workshops, but perhaps particularly this one, it's important that you prepare yourself emotionally. Be sure you are both in a good mood. The underlying stratum, the deepest level within yourselves, has to be receptive to change or the session will go nowhere.

You want to talk about money. You want to clarify things between you. You have been able to temporarily put aside hurt and anger.

You are prepared to listen to your partner and let them tell it as it is for them. You understand the point is not to get angry or defensive, but to take the differences between you and shape them into a working partnership.

STEP #1: Who Are You In Your Dreams?

What's your secret wish? Your dream? Is a little money enough, or do you want a big pile? You need to know the financial goal you have for yourself. You need to know if it is the same goal your partner has.

Tell your partner how you would like to live. Be explicit as to the role money plays.

The closer your dream styles, the more easily you will get along, but no one is "wrong" or to blame if you have different lifestyles in mind. It's just that if your styles are too far apart, you're going to have some heavy work to do to come together. For example, if one of you envisions a table set with sterling silver and Waterford crystal, and one of you envisions a modest cottage on a windswept shore in Maine, you're going to have nothing but trouble ahead. In fact, you probably have a lot of trouble right now.

Do you share the same vision for the future, or do you have something different in mind? You need to see how your view of the future fits with your partner's view, and then you need to know if you share the same ideas as to how to get there. Are you alike or very different in how you handle money? What is your financial style?

STEP #2: Your Money Style

Are you a spendthrift or a tightwad? Do you have to buy something the minute you see it, or can you wait until you can afford it? Do you prefer to pay with cash or use a credit card? Is the size of your diamond ring more important than the savings in the bank? Would you prefer to live for the moment or save for the future?

Lots of trouble can come up when two people who manage one pile of money have different styles. When the differences are discussed, you can agree to compromise by meeting each other halfway.

Take turns telling your partner how you would like to see your joint money managed. Be as frank and open as you can.

For example, if your partner is a saver, can you reassure him that you have no intention of bankrupting him? Can you let him know you really hear his concerns about money? Can you let him know you're with him, not against him?

Or if your partner is a spender, how can you reassure her that your goal is not to restrict her? How can you give her a freer rein? How can you let her know you want the same good things for her that she wants?

I can hear your responses: "So, let him control me? We'd never do anything or get anything!" Or, "So, let her bankrupt me? Am I crazy?"

If indeed these are the thoughts that come to your mind, pause a moment. If your partner would really try to control you or bankrupt you, your problem is far different than money. Your problem is how your partner regards you. Your partner may say they love you, but how is that tied in with the respect they have for you? With their willingness to treat you as an equal person when it actually comes down to money?

STEP #3: The Power Balance

Money and power—often the two go hand in hand. The partner who has more money has more freedom, more independence. I overhead a comment once: "In a relationship, the power belongs to the person who can leave more easily." The statement was in regard to emotions, but it is true in regard to money as well. The partner who has the most money is often the one who can leave most easily.

Too little money can erode and destroy a relationship, but too much money can be a problem as well. The old adage that power corrupts is as true at home as it is in politics, and restoring an equal power-money balance can be vital to your relationship. It is well worth the effort.

Say to your partner, "I think of you as an equal. I want to be honest with you, open, and fair to you. I love you and want to share the good things in life with you."

If you are the main income provider, resolve to allow your partner full participation in financial decisions. Think of them as truly equal.

STEP #4: Women's New Role

Although it can always be a problem when one partner earns more than the other, it can be particularly difficult if it is a woman who earns more than a man. Such an unequal balance calls for maturity and sensitivity on the part of both partners in dealing with the feelings that may arise.

Say to your partner: "Our relationship means more to me than money ever can. I truly respect and appreciate your efforts to keep this imbalance from causing conflict between us. Please tell me what I can do to keep this from hurting our relationship."

Whatever the problem, remember: if you can talk about it, you have a good chance of resolving it!

STEP #5: *Fairness In Love And War*

Fairness in relationships has a lot to do with the distribution of work. Who gets to work? Who gets to play? Exactly who is carrying the biggest burden? Exactly who is working the hardest?

I have had the working partner say to me, "It's not fair! I have to go to work every day. She gets to stay home and have fun!" And I have had stay-at-home partners say, "It's not fair! He gets to go to the quiet of his office every day, but I have to stay home and deal with the chaos of children and housework!"

In any relationship, it's important to make your partner feel that the distribution of work is fair. Unfairness breeds conflict and unhappiness. Say to your partner, "I want to be fair to you. Do you think I have been? Tell me how I can improve. Do you think we share the money equally? Do we share the work equally? Do you feel you work harder than I? Do you think I have it easier than you?" And, finally, ask the question: "How can we even it out?"

When your partner answers, LISTEN. Don't try to put what you think forward; instead, try to understand how they see things. Get their view for a change. Don't instantly respond. Give yourself time to think about what they've said. Do they have a point? Where could you give a little more, balance things out a little more, or just be a little more appreciative of what they do?

STEP #6: *Money and Deceit*

Sometimes the situation is worse than just "unfairness"; sometimes one partner is actually deceiving the other. It's surprising how many people who would never take advantage of a partner in the business world will, without a second thought, take terrible advantage of their mate. As though the license to love also includes a license to take.

There are people who deceive their partners, not only in regard to love but in regard to money. Perhaps they sock it away on the side or secretly spend it. Even more common, they just don't share vital information.

I've had several instances in which when one partner's signature is needed (say, for a loan or to buy property), the other partner just forges it. The deceit isn't found out until long after the fact. Often this deceit goes unnoticed until some chance event reveals it, or until financial disaster hits the family.

Is such deceit worth the price you pay? You're deceiving the person you love, your life partner. Is that really what you want? Is the dishonesty worth the gain? I don't think so!

You may say in defense, "But I'm worried about the future: the relationship may change. I may get left. I may want to leave."

True. Relationships don't last forever. People die. People change. But isn't there a better way to deal with that than to be dishonest and secretive? Doesn't that in itself contribute to a self-fulfilling prophecy of disaster?

If you have been dishonest or deceitful in your relationship regarding money, decide to put an end to that. Make the decision privately unless it's important that your partner know. If you need to tell your partner, say to them as a start, "I have kept things from you in regard to our finances. I'm truly sorry. I love you and I want to clean the slate and make a new beginning. Please help me do that."

Work out with your partner a plan of action. Document on paper the steps you will take.

STEP #7: Closing The Session

It is the end of the session. Have you been able to talk about money? Have you opened up areas that were closed? Do you each feel okay about it? Is there more work to do?

If so, schedule a time for another session. In the interim, write down the points you want to bring up. Bring them to the next session.

Part II

Sexual Intimacy

Chapter 7

Couples And Sex

Women complain about sex more often than men. Their gripes fall into two major categories: (1) Not enough (2) Too much.

—Ann Landers, *Truth is Stranger than Fiction*

Some sexual conflicts are major, some minor, but all tap into the heart of a relationship, because even when the hurt seems trivial, when it is sexual, it is not easily forgiven or forgotten.

Are you, as an individual, hoarding a secret sexual hurt? Are you, as a couple, having a problem with sex?

Good sex adds to your power as a couple, but bad sex weakens and divides you. Bad sex leaves you with a feeling of loneliness and isolation, and can lead to a depressed state that affects your entire life.

Most Couples Have Trouble with Sex

Although sex may have been what brought you together, it can easily turn into what drives you apart. The main reason for this is not that sex itself is so difficult, but that our culture gives very confusing messages as to what sex is and what it should be.

Since sex is something so closely tied to your feelings and self-esteem, it can be very difficult to talk about. One purpose of this chapter is to give you a place to talk about and deal with the most intimate part of your life.

Most Couples Have Trouble Talking about Sex

If you can't talk about something, it's very unlikely that you can change it. Can you talk with your partner about sex? Not sex in the abstract, but sex as it directly affects your relationship?

When the problem is sexual, how do you break the ice and say what you may have long kept silent? The words you use are important, but even more important is the way you say them. And even more important than that is the way your partner hears them. The most important step in coming together has to do with the attitude you bring to each other.

Breaking the Ice: Your Attitude

If you're having a problem with sex, the first step is to shift from seeing your partner as the problem to seeing your sexual interaction as the problem. You want to attack the problem, not each other. You have nothing to lose by taking the first step and letting go of the struggle against each other.

The following chapters deal with separate, specific aspects of sex, but the focus of this chapter is to help you as a couple to start working on the problem as allies. If you're fighting each other, there's no way to win. The purpose of this chapter is to help you get on the same side of the conflict.

Getting on the Same Side of the Conflict

Sex is viewed very differently by different people. How you were raised, what you were taught, what you've experienced—it all makes a difference. In fact, just being a man or a woman will probably make a difference as to how you view sex. It's as if you see sex through different ends of the telescope, or, to put it another way, you're on different trips, heading for different destinations.

This doesn't have to be the case.

It's quite possible, and very helpful, to lay out certain basic concepts about sex that you can share. Agreeing on these concepts is a way of getting on the same side of the conflict. Then you know at least that you're starting from the same place, talking about the same thing, and heading in the same direction.

What Is Sex?

Contrary to what you may think, this seemingly direct and simple question is a very difficult one to answer. This is one reason why so many couples have difficulty with sex. We each have our own way of conceptualizing it, what we think it should be, and what we want it to be.

Think back to President Bill Clinton's famous response, in the press conference of January 1998, when he stated, "I did not have sexual relations with that woman,"—a statement many would not agree with. (If you are interested, you actually can view Bill Clinton saying this on YouTube).

In looking for a definition as to "What is sex?" we find dictionaries are of little help, since current thinking has so broadened the field that most such definitions are obsolete. The Internet gives more up-to-date information:

> The word sex is used to refer to a variety of sexual activities, and can mean different things to different people. When people talk about sex (sexual intercourse) they are usually referring to penetrative sex, where a man inserts his penis into the vagina or anus of a sexual partner.
>
> However, there are many sexual activities that people enjoy doing which don't involve sexual intercourse, for example oral sex or mutual masturbation.

The act of sex is also not just physical; it can involve strong emotions and have a significant effect on people's feelings.[4]

So there we have an answer, but not a simple answer. Just as sexual activities can mean different things to different people, so sexual interaction for couples is an individual matter and can include a variety of sexual activities.

The important thing is that this interaction be successful. That is, that it brings sexual gratification to each partner, increasing their sense of closeness and strengthening their relationship.

The question then becomes, "How is such sexual gratification achieved?"

Sexual gratification is achieved when the need for physical closeness and intimacy is satisfied. It's that simple. Sexual gratification occurs when your need to be intimate and touched by your partner is fulfilled.

For most of us, sex has become entangled with our self-image, feelings of right and wrong, a need to be loved, fears of rejection. Can you put all of that aside for now? Can you see sexual gratification as simply fulfillment of a basic need we all have to be touched, to be intimately close to another, to no longer be physically alone?

Sexual Gratification Is Achieved Primarily Through the Sense of Touch

There is nothing mysterious about sex. It's quite simply the mutual caressing and stimulating of physical

---

4   http://www.avert.org/sex-questions.htm

receptors in the skin, particularly in the genital area. The experience can reach the level of sexual climax, but does not have to.

If you're willing to let yourself feel and enjoy touch, you can enjoy sex. If you're willing to touch and caress your partner, you can give sexual pleasure. If you are willing to let your partner touch and caress you, you can receive sexual gratification. The pleasure, however, should not just be an occasional or chance occurrence; it needs to be the heart of the experience.

Regardless of the emotional complexities you bring to your relationship, if you're willing, it's within your power to touch and accept the body of your partner. It's within your power, if you're willing, to give them sexual gratification, and it's within your power as well to enjoy the sense of touch and intimacy.

After all, isn't that what you would like: the knowledge that you are wanted and accepted physically? And isn't that what you would like to give your partner: the surety of knowing that they also are wanted and appreciated physically?

When sex is viewed this way (a simple need for physical closeness and intimacy), it's not so very different from any of the other needs (or drives) that you deal with every day of your life.

For example, you've probably been able to come together in regard to eating: when you eat, what you eat, and how you eat. Why not the same with sex? And you've probably been able to come together as to sleeping:

when you sleep and how you sleep. Why not the same with sex?

When you can think of sex as a simple physical interchange that brings sensual pleasure to each partner, it'll be easier to deal with. You'll have taken away its power and cut it down to size.

Sex Is Learned

Why do you have to learn how to have sex? The reason is that, although you may be born with the drive that leads to having sex, you are not born knowing how to have sex. You are not born knowing how to touch your partner.

Each person is different; each person's response to touch is different. When you have sex with a partner, you have to learn how to fulfill their sensual need to be touched. You need to learn how to touch them.

There is one condition, however, that must be fulfilled before you can enjoy touch. That is: you have to feel safe. You have to be in a safe "holding environment," which means you know you are with someone who cares about you, someone who is accepting of you, someone who would never hurt or ridicule you.

Your caring about each other is more important than sex. If it were primarily sex you were interested in, you could find that elsewhere. What you really want is to have good sex with this partner because you love and want to please them.

The Primary Goal of Sex Is Pleasure

Sex can have many goals: to please your partner, to get pregnant, to release sexual tension, to affirm the fact that you're desirable, etc. All of these may be important, but to make the sexual act itself successful, one goal needs to be primary: pleasure.

When you agree to make pleasure the primary goal, you agree also to let go of all other goals, both for yourself and for your partner. For example, if pleasure is the primary goal, it really doesn't matter whether you reach orgasm. It doesn't matter whether you are old or young. It doesn't matter whether you are rich or poor. It doesn't matter whether you are fat or thin. The only requirement for each of you is that you try to give your partner sensual pleasure, and that you find such pleasure for yourself as well.

Do you agree (more or less) with the above comments? Can you add some of your own? If so, you are ready for the workshop, which will guide you in breaking the ice and talking about sex. Good luck!

The Workshop

You have set a time and found a place that is quiet and in which you will not be interrupted. The topic is sex. You are ready to begin.

STEP #1: Letting Go Of The Struggle Against Each Other

The feelings you bring to the session have everything to do with how the session will go. If you're defensive, angry, out to prove your partner wrong, the session will be a failure.

In order to talk about sex, you need to create an atmosphere that is safe. You must assure your partner that what you say is not said to hurt, anger, embarrass, or humiliate them. You must assure your partner that you want to hear what they have to say.

You need to know from your partner: You will not hurt me. You will not leave me. I can say things to you and you will not hold them against me forever. I can say things to you and I know they are confidential. You will not betray me by telling others.

Say to your partner, "I love you. I have no desire to hurt you. My whole purpose in saying anything to you is to make our relationship better."

Take turns saying this. Have you been able to say the words with meaning despite whatever hurt or anger you may have been feeling? Do you feel safe with each other? If so, you are ready to go on to Step 2.

STEP #2: *Learning About Each Other*

Although you may be very close, or have lived together a long time, you still may be in the dark as to how you feel about sex. Or, if you have talked about it, it has probably been in a guarded way, half-truths to protect yourself, or your partner, from embarrassment.

Take fifteen minutes each and give your partner a brief background as to how you learned about sex and what your family's attitudes were.

This does not mean you are to tell everything. Be careful as to what you share. Don't share something harmful to your partner. Some things are private. Some things are hurtful. Share those things that you feel would be helpful for your partner to know about you.

Perhaps this leads to a discussion that lasts the whole hour. If so, continue at the next session; if not, take a few minutes and give your partner a brief summary of how you view your past sexual experience.

You don't need to know a lot about each other's past, but it's helpful to have a general idea. If you're both virgins, your experience with each other will be quite different and the expectations different than if you both have had many sexual relationships.

Again, use good common sense when you share. If you have never been sensitive to others, begin now.

Would you like to hear details of your partner's previous affairs or old boyfriends? Probably not. Would it help for your partner to know that you've had an abortion? Again, probably not. However, each situation is different, and being honest and forthright with each other creates a clean slate on which to begin your relationship.

Perhaps it would help to know that your partner had a long love affair that ended in abandonment, or that your partner has had many relationships but this is the first serious commitment in which marriage is a possibility. You may find your backgrounds are similar, or they may be far apart. What's important is that you can be understanding and accepting of the differences between you.

STEP #3: What Do You Want From Sex?

What role do you want sex to play in your life? What do you think a good sexual relationship is? What do you think the goal of sex should be? The more you share similar goals and expectations, the greater your chances for happiness.

Take turns and tell your partner what, in your fantasy, you would like sex to be.

Do you feel orgasm is essential? In your fantasy, do you want your partner to do certain things, touch you in a certain way, be a certain way? Can you describe this to them?

Do you feel the most important part of sex is being caressed and told you are attractive? Do you want to be adored and told so? If so, tell your partner.

Your fantasies can be very different. If you know each other's fantasies, then you can move to satisfy them. If you know your differences, you can work to resolve them.

Again, perhaps this discussion has filled the hour; if so, schedule another session. If not, continue with Step 4.

STEP #4: Identifying The Ways You Differ From Each Other

Make a list of what you see as the major sexual differences between you. Discuss the differences or similarities. Might they relate to some of the problems you have?

For example, one of you would like sex once a week, and one of you would like sex every night. How can you compromise? Is there a middle ground?

One of you would like mainly just to be held, and one of you wants intercourse and just intercourse. Is it possible to combine and expand your lovemaking so each partner feels satisfied?

One of you is fearful of pregnancy, and one of you would really like another baby. Aren't you at cross purposes? Isn't this something that needs talking about? Perhaps you should consider reading the chapter on "Couples and Children."

One of you feels a lack of love and "just used" when you have sex, and one of you feels physically rejected when you don't have sex. Aren't you misunderstanding each other? How can you have good sex when you are each feeling hurt and angry?

You can't expect to resolve your differences in one session. You can expect, once you know what your differences are, to begin to work on them. If you have been able to break the ice and identify some of the problems, you are off to a good start.

Chapter 8

Couples, Sex, And Sensation
Or
Behind Closed Doors

The energy generated by what happens "behind closed doors" has a great deal to do with how you feel about yourself, and a great deal to do with how you feel as a couple. The power of sex, cloaked within the lure of falling in love, is often the force, or the energy, that has brought you together.

Sexual power works for you when its sources, the body and the mind, are in harmony. The two, although inseparable, are quite distinct. It's through your body that you make actual physical contact with your partner. It's through your mind that you assess and bring meaning to the experience.

It's through your body, the actual nerve endings of your skin, that the sensation of sexual, sensual pleasure is perceived. It is here that the action is. I had a man tell me after his divorce, "Physically, I need sex. I miss it! What am I to do?" I had a recently widowed woman tell me, "It's as if my whole body is crying out to be held. I physically ache with longing!"

This ache is a body ache, a physical yearning to be touched. When you were an infant, fulfillment of this need was necessary for life itself. It goes back to the very roots of your experience. Did you know that babies in an orphanage, even though they are fed and given shelter, will waste away and die if they are not touched?[5] One of the joys of being a couple is that you have found someone with whom to share this basic sensual need. You are not alone! You have a partner! Why, then, do things so often go wrong?

What's Gone Wrong?

Maybe you've read all the books or seen explicit videos. Perhaps you've even had counseling or reached a point where you feel hopeless about yourself. No one else seems to have a problem with sex; it must be you.

---

5   "Emotional Deprivation in Infancy," Study by Rene A. Spitz, 1952

No, it's not just you! It's that you, like many others, have an underlying backlog of experience that gets in the way of your being the sexually responsive person you want to be. The reason for this is not complicated. If you were raised as a child in a family where genital self-touch is forbidden (and many people have), it will not be easy to suddenly become a freely touching and sensuous sexual partner.

If you were raised in a family where shame over body functions was intense (and many have), you'll not be able to suddenly become an active, responsive sexual partner.

No way! Just because the culture you live in is obsessed with sex, just because talk shows tell everything, and just because how-to books on sex are everywhere doesn't mean you, yourself, when you go to have sex, are going to be suddenly free of a lifetime of prohibitions.

No. On the contrary, it's going to take a conscious effort to change and reintegrate within yourself an accepting view not only of your own sexuality but also of that of your partner. You need to give yourself permission: It's okay to touch! It's okay to be touched!

Women and Touch

Both men and women have been taught from childhood not to "touch" themselves, but the admonition for women is more powerful. Little girls are supposed to be nice. And sweet. And pretty. None of these adjectives apply to having sex, and this is a contradiction that remains a problem for many women throughout their lives.

How does a "nice" little girl transition to a "sexy" woman? How does the image of being a mother mesh with that of being "sexy"?

Little girls are still being raised today with powerful prohibitions against sex, and, strangely enough, the prohibitor is most often the mother. It's mothers who say "don't touch" when their daughters are little, and mothers who fear their daughters having sex when they are older. An unwanted pregnancy can still bring disgrace on an entire family, as well as financial hardship.

In my practice I've seen many women who've had a teenage pregnancy and an abortion. For many of these women, the most terrifying part of this experience was having to tell their mother. The shame of this telling can last a lifetime, and no matter how sophisticated you may be, the memory can block full sexual response.

Men and Touch

It's not only women who have a problem with touch. Men do as well. In fact, the inability to enjoy touch may be even more of a problem for men than it is for women. One reason for this is that it's a hidden problem. Men are quick to recognize that a woman has a problem if she doesn't "feel" anything during sex (she's "frigid"), but often they are totally unaware of their own inability to feel.

Jack, a man in his fifties, bragged about himself: "I've had lots of sexual affairs," he said, "but I want you to know I've never touched myself!" Jack is Catholic. He learned as a child that touching himself is a sin. He is proud that he has never masturbated. In all the love affairs he's had, he's never allowed a woman to touch him, and he never manually touches a woman. What kind of pleasure can he allow himself? What kind of a lover must he be?

Another man, Bill, brought to the session by his wife because she felt distanced by him sexually, said, "I can't stand body contact. I love my wife, but if she wants to cuddle, I get hot and sweaty and anxious right away. I have to move." He added, "And I don't like to be touched—other than genitally. It's always felt more like tickling—unpleasant. I just don't enjoy it." Bill has a prohibition against touching. In his mind, the pleasure of touch (other than genital) is a self-indulgence that a "real" man wouldn't enjoy.

Many men, like Jack and Bill, have never allowed themselves to enjoy whole-body touching. Only the phallic act of penetration is permitted. By limiting feeling to the penis, men can hold themselves aloof, separate. Then they are safe from what might otherwise be a frightening regression to an infantile state of merging with another.

Women, lacking a penis, respond with their entire bodies, their "whole" self. The man who confines his feeling to his penis is less vulnerable than the woman who, by the very nature of her whole-body response, is more fully involved.

Men who are unaware of the pleasures of touch don't enjoy foreplay. Foreplay is something they "do" for their partner, not for themselves. Often they find it boring or tedious. They really don't know how to include the woman as a partner and have sex with her. They don't even know what they are missing, and they have no idea that they are a poor sexual partner.

How to Learn to Feel

If you were a child who was taught that touching is wrong and the pleasure derived from touching is sinful, enjoying sex is not going to be easy. You must rethink your receptivity to touch. You must give yourself permission to feel, not just genitally but with your whole body. When your partner touches you and you feel their body close to you, instead of pulling away, you need to relax. You need to let your skin feel and enjoy the closeness. Once you can open the door to your own feeling, you will begin to appreciate your partner's pleasure as well. You'll be on the path to becoming a good lover.

In order to change, you talk to your mind (which, interestingly enough, will hear what you say) and tell yourself sex is "okay." You tell yourself that sex is an activity forbidden to children but not to adults. You are an adult. You not only can but should now enjoy touch!

You also tell yourself that, never having really allowed yourself to feel, you need to give yourself time to learn to feel. You are going to have to reteach yourself. You have to say to yourself, "Touching is not bad. I have a right to feel. I will allow myself to feel."

Sensation won't come all at once. You need to know that it takes a conscious effort. It will take work to learn to feel.

Centering

"Centering" is an important part of feeling. The act of centering is a conscious focusing on what is happening at the moment. Women must let go of the responsibilities they carry, be that making up a grocery list, planning the next meal, worrying about a sick child, or running a business. You must clear all else from your mind if you are to enjoy your partner's touch.

Men may have an easier time centering since the focus is already on their penis; however, what some men do worry about is the sex itself. After all, they are the ones who have to perform! They worry: Am I going to lose my erection? or, Is she going to have an orgasm?

Sam kept asking his wife, Rita, "Have you had one? Did you have an orgasm?" Rita told me she was so pressured by his concern that she couldn't relax and enjoy the lovemaking. Her orgasm, she said, was a measure of his success. This put a great weight on her.

"Actually," she said, "sometimes I have an orgasm; sometimes I don't. It's no big deal for me. I just wish he'd forget about it and think about himself." Sam needs to focus on his feelings, not on his anxieties and concerns. He needs to "center" on the physical, sensual experience itself.

Perhaps an analogy to food is helpful. The pleasure in eating has to reside in the satisfaction of your own taste experience. It's not selfish to enjoy your own sense of taste, nor is it selfish to center on your own sexual pleasure. It's necessary.

Just as with a good meal, however, your partner's enjoyment is very important as well. You get pleasure from their pleasure, and if they are not happy, it takes away from your enjoyment as well.

Where to Touch

Since touch is so important, you have to know where to touch; you need to know a little bit about anatomy. It's hard to feel confident about what you're doing if you're in a strange land, and women's anatomy seems a strange and mysterious land to many men. It really helps to know the "lay of the land."

The Lay of the Land

The first time a man has intercourse, how is he supposed to know where the vagina is? Is it close to the urethra? Or to the clitoris? What is the clitoris, anyway? And exactly where is it? Mystery after mystery!

Today the Internet can help remove much of this mystery, but, still, doing something for the first time in person is quite different than reading about it online.

Charles, a young man who came to see me, told me that the first time he had intercourse he thought women had "just one hole down there." In fact, even after intercourse, he still wasn't sure at all of just what was what or where "down there." Charles had the notion that everyone else knew about these things—only he was ignorant.

But Charles is not alone in regard to not knowing about female anatomy. A lot of men are ignorant. Part of the problem is they've never been told, and part of the problem is that every woman's anatomy is a little different. What most, if not all, men need is help from their partner in the actual act of having sex.

Women also need help from their partner. Again, despite knowledge from friends or the Internet, when it comes to one's own first experience, it is a different matter. For women raised in a traditional household, or not having brothers, or with parents of another generation, seeing a penis for the first time in person can be quite a shock. It is an immense organ, and one they don't have. One woman said to me, "It seemed grotesque at first—like a sixth finger in the wrong place!" If a woman is not experienced sexually, she needs help in knowing that it's okay to touch, that in fact this is something the man desires very much.

In the workshop that follows, you will be guided as you talk to your partner about touch and your response to touch. The goal is to find out what your partner would like from you, and for you to be able to tell your partner what you would like from them. However, it is one thing to talk about sex in general, but it's quite another to talk about it as it affects you directly.

Phrase what you say as carefully as you can, but don't be afraid to say it. Try not to be offended or hurt by what your partner says. Remember, even if something is upsetting to you, isn't it still better to know? Remaining ignorant solves nothing, but if you have knowledge as to what the problem is, you can work to change it.

This is your chance to speak for yourself. Encourage your partner to speak openly as well. Be as supportive of them and what they have to say as you would like them to be of you.

Today, many good "how-to" books on sex are available. The new edition of *The Joy of Sex*[6] is outstanding and is updated both as to male and female perspectives. I recommend it to you as an adjunct to the workshop that follows.

---

6   *The Joy of Sex: The Timeless Guide to Lovemaking, Ultimate Revised Edition,* Alex Comfort and Susan Quilliam (Jan 2009)

The Workshop

STEP #1: Beginning The Workshop

Talk about touching in your childhood and in your family. Take turns and tell your partner how you feel about being touched. Do you like it or does it make you feel uneasy? Is touch and touching something that comes easy to you?

For example, did your parents openly touch and caress each other?

What about you? Did you get hugged and kissed growing up? Too little? Too much? Are you self-conscious about touching? Did your family "kiss the air" instead of your cheek or lips? Did your dad put his arm around you and give you a hug now and then? Or did your family frown on any physical demonstration of affection? All of this information is important in understanding both yourself and your partner's ability to enjoy touching and being touched.

STEP #2: Do You Have Some Fears About Touching?

Are you embarrassed to touch or be touched? Have you had bad experiences in regard to touch? Were you ever caught touching yourself (masturbating)? If so, what happened? Did the experience leave you with a fear of touching? Take turns. Listen quietly as your partner tells you their experiences.

Although most hang-ups in regard to touch can be worked on on your own as a couple, certain problems do need professional help. Perhaps you were inappropriately touched or overstimulated sexually as a child. In this particular situation, I recommend you delay the workshop until you have a chance to work with a therapist and have resolved some of the emotional blocks this can cause. It really isn't fair to your partner to put something so emotionally heavy on them alone. Indeed, they too may need professional help in dealing with such trauma.

STEP #3: *What Part Of You Do You Most Like Being Touched? Take Turns And Try To Be As Open As Possible.*

For example, do you like your back rubbed? Tickled? Your feet massaged? Do you like it when your penis is touched? When your testicles are touched? When your breasts and nipples are touched? What about your anus? Is this pleasurable or embarrassing for you? Do you have feeling in the vagina, or just the clitoris? Where is it most pleasurable for you to be touched?

STEP #4: *If You Feel Ready, Tell Your Partner How You Would Like Them To Touch You.*

Try to be specific.

Some people have what used to be called "hot" spots, and they are so sensitive there, touching is not pleasant.

Some people like gentle touching, some people like firmer touching. People are all different.

Time can make a difference, too. For example, some people like touching and sex in the morning. Others are totally out of the mood and get very irritated if touched when they are still half asleep. It helps to tell your partner openly if such is the case rather than just inwardly groaning and putting up with it.

STEP #5: Tell Your Partner How You Feel About Touching Them.

Do you like to touch your partner? Are you bored? Restless? Or is it fun? Nice? Intimate? Sexually arousing? Are you afraid of being rejected? Are you timid? Are you afraid to touch your partner because you don't know how?

One woman told me of an experience that had totally inhibited her touching her husband. Early in their relationship, being very daring, she had reached over and touched his testicles. She thought she had been gentle, but he suddenly leaped up with a shout of pain! She apologized profusely but, despite his reassurance that "it was nothing," she was so intimidated she never touched his testicles again.

STEP #6: No Words To Use

Recently I saw a young woman, Jennifer, who complained that her husband didn't know where to touch her when they had sex, and when he did have the right place, he pressed too hard. When I asked, "Why didn't you tell him?" she said, "I'm too embarrassed. Plus, I don't have any words to use. Clitoris! Labia! Ugh!"

We both laughed at the "Ugh," but she was quite right. We don't have a language that feels natural to use when talking about sex. So how could Jennifer tell her husband what she wanted? What, of course, she might have done would be to have taken his hand and shown him what she wanted.

You may be wondering why she had to be told something so obvious. She had to be told because many, perhaps most, women have gotten the message that it's not okay to be the leader in lovemaking. In fact, not only is it not okay, it can be very risky. Women have learned that men can be "turned off" abruptly if the wrong thing is said or done, and some men actually become insulted or angry.

Fortunately, in this case, when Jennifer took her husband's hand and showed him exactly where she wanted to be touched, he was simply delighted. You, too, need to be delighted if your partner is courageous enough to show you exactly how and where to touch them.

Being unable to talk about sex is a handicap. If you are too embarrassed to talk about sex, or don't know words to use, try the following exercise. You may feel foolish doing it, but it can indeed break the ice and allow you to begin to communicate with your partner. Give it a try; it can't hurt!

Take turns and say aloud to each other ten times:

- CLITORIS
- VAGINA
- PENIS
- LABIA
- SCROTUM
- TESTICLE
- NIPPLE
- ORGASM
- ANUS

These are all terms that are not an easy part of speech. They are "loaded" words, by which I mean they carry extra emotional baggage that makes them hard to use. Some people can't even say "nipple" without a twinge of unease. By saying these "forbidden" words aloud, many times over, you are breaking the ice and can probably laugh about whatever inhibitions you have.

There is a world of slang out there now that substitutes for these words. A good place to find them is "The Online Slang Dictionary."[7] For some, slang can be easier to break the ice with than traditional words. Some couples even have slang of their own, just to be used in their special relationship.

Whatever words you choose, the goal is to be comfortable talking to each other about sex.

---

7   http://onlineslangdictionary.com

STEP #7: *Finishing The Workshop*

Do you feel you can talk to each other about touching? If not, schedule another workshop to continue working on it. Don't be in a hurry! You have probably had the problems for a long time, and it's only reasonable to assume that some more time will be needed for them to change.

Chapter 9

Sex And Psyche (Mind)[8]

There is nothing either good or bad, but thinking
makes it so.

—Shakespeare, *Hamlet*

You may have heard people say, "Sex is all in your
mind," and to some extent that is so. Body and mind
are inextricably connected; one cannot exist without
the other. When sex is good, there is a sense of mental

---

8   *"Psyche" as used in a psychiatric sense as "the Mind." Although the words
psyche and mind technically mean the same thing, for me, psyche has a slightly
broader connotation—a little more ethereal and spiritual. Here, however, I will be
using the terms interchangeably.*

well-being. Your energy is increased, and you feel a power not only in your relationship but in your whole life.

One of my patients, Annette described her feelings this way: "When we wake up and have sex in the morning, I go to work feeling great. I feel as if I'm walking on air, as if I could do anything. I feel complete. I feel whole. I feel as if I have a wonderful secret inside. The secret is: someone made love to me this morning!

On the other hand, when sex is not good, it casts a shadow on your whole life. Something is missing; something is not right between you and the person who means the most to you in all the world. All day, every day, you carry a feeling within you that things are not as they should be, or could be, between you and your partner. Such unhappiness may well underlie much of the depression doctors try to cure with a pill. Sometimes the pill will dull the pain, but the pill alone will not make the problem go away.

Sheila and Eric had been married for eight years when Sheila came to see me because she was considering divorce. "We tried to make love last night. It was awful! I thought he didn't really want to but felt obligated." She paused, "To be truthful, I didn't want to either."

Then she added, "Something is wrong with us. We're a failure sexually. Eric is unhappy, and I find myself crying, sometimes just out of the blue. I tried Prozac for awhile, but it just seemed to dull the edge. The pain was gone, but the problem was still there."

In the previous chapter, the focus was on your body and how, if you can allow yourself to physically feel through the sense of touch, you will inevitably have a sexual response. However, you are not just a set of nerves responding to stimuli. You are a thinking, emotionally responsive human being whose mind has the power to open or close the door to sexual feelings. Before you can respond sexually to your partner, your mind must be ready.

The Power of Your Mind

Your mind (your psyche) has the power to turn you on to sex. Fantasy alone can arouse intense desire and actual physical response. Unfortunately, your mind also has the power to turn you off to sex. Mind blocks, conscious and unconscious, can stop the normal flow of sexual energy and can keep you from being the sexual partner you would like to be.

Mind Blocks

There are many mind blocks you can work on on your own. In the workshop, you will be asked, "Do you think something is blocking your ability to be as responsive sexually as you would like?" If the answer is yes, you will be asked to try to identify it. Let me give you some examples of common mind blocks:

1. Is Sex Really Okay?

You'd be surprised at how many people really don't think sex is okay. They, of course, don't ask anyone, "Is sex really okay?" But when they attempt to have sex, or respond a little more freely than they usually do, they hear this little voice way in the background saying, "Is this really okay?"

The doubt is there: Do nice people really do this? Probably this voice is louder for women than for men. Women have been taught since childhood to be "nice," or they risk not being loved.

Men never were supposed to be "nice"; however, they can be very ambivalent toward women who are not "nice," that is, toward women who are really sexual. Although men may encourage women in every way to be sexual, when they are, men may have doubts. Robert Wright, in his book *The Moral Animal,* [9] even goes so far as to suggest that when a man is ready for a commitment, he will shy away from a woman who is "too sexy," believing she's really not good "mother material."

2. Is This Really Love?

If you think, I love this person; it's okay to have sex together, your mind opens the gate to feeling. If you think, Do I love this person? Should I? Shouldn't I? the gate to sexual feeling opens and closes. At one time you may feel turned on, at another turned off.

---

9   Robert Wright, *The Moral Animal: Why We Are the Way We Are: The New Science of Evolutionary Psychology*, Vintage, 1995

Love and sex are two different things. Love is a powerful emotion experienced by your mind. Sex is a physical act over in a short time. The arbitrary tying together of love and sex can lead to many problems.

When you have doubt in your mind, you give only a part of yourself. You're holding back, and this may be partly because of a fantasy that has long outgrown its usefulness, or perhaps because of a recent conflict that has left angry feelings. Such angry feelings can also be a mind block.

3. Anger Can Be a Mind Block to Having Sex

You may ask, "How can I have sex when I'm angry with my partner? Having sex isn't something I want to do at all!"

Anger keeps many couples apart. Withholding sex can become a way of punishing your partner, a way of expressing anger. This is a destructive mind block, however, that seldom acts as effective punishment. But it does serve to keep you apart, and it does, in itself, often increase the anger.

The point is not that you should have sex regardless of feelings. The point is that to make an idealized state of feeling a certain way a precondition to having sex can do more harm than good. If you have anger toward your partner, it's better to deal with it directly than to act it out through a withholding of sex. After all, isn't withholding sex a punishment for you as well?

4. Sexual Fantasies versus Reality

Fantasies can enhance sexual feelings by creating a desire for sex or filling a void when sex is absent;

however, when fantasies are out-of-touch with reality they can cause a problem.

Jim had a fantasy that once you were married you could have sex every night. He and Sue did have sex every night for the first six months of their marriage, but then after the first baby arrived this decreased to two-three times a week, and then, after the second baby, once a week.

Jim was disappointed, hurt, and angry. When he would confront Sue about why she didn't want to have sex every night, she would burst into tears and wouldn't talk with him. Feelings had reached a point that neither of them even wanted to have sex.

"My wife doesn't love me as I love her," he told me. "I am even thinking of having an affair."

Sue said she did indeed love him, but she was exhausted, and his demand for sex every night was simply too much for her. Their two daughters were now six months and two years. Sue did all the housekeeping, cooking, and necessary shopping. She also worked part-time as a receptionist at a small nearby shop and wanted to continue. She said she was so upset when Jim had confronted her by saying he didn't feel she loved him as much as he loved her that all she could do was cry.

In the session they worked on many aspects of their relationship, but Jim's letting go of his fantasy that they should have sex every night, and taking into account the reality of the situation, improved their relationship greatly.

5. An Earlier Love

Sometimes it's not just a fantasy that may be holding you back and blocking sexual feelings but a memory of a real person. Perhaps you have a shadowy memory of an earlier love, and this remains to interfere with your full sexual response now.

Bill had remarried a year after his wife's death. Their marriage had been a happy one, and her death had been very difficult for him. He felt very fortunate to have found Jan, his new wife, who was a lovely, animated woman. They had had sex right from the beginning of their relationship, and at first it had been great, but now that they were married and Jan had moved into his home, everything came to a stop. Bill had no interest in sex. When they did have sex, it was at Jan's initiative and was not satisfactory for either of them.

The reason for the problem seemed clear. The "presence" of Bill's former wife was a mind block that stopped all of Bill's interest in sex. In Bill's mind, Jan had replaced his wife, living in "her" house, sleeping in "her" bed, having sex with "her" husband. Bill even had pictures of his former wife throughout the house.

One of the steps Bill and Jan took to fix this problem was to move to a house of their own. In addition, Bill had to consciously put aside his memories of his first wife. He had to give himself full permission to have sex with Jan.

6. Am I Attractive Sexually?

Both men and women worry about this. This conscious fear can spoil the best of relationships and is a mind block for many. Men worry their penis is too small. Women worry about everything: I'm too old. I'm too fat. My breasts are too small. My hips are too large. I have stretch marks. For women, in particular, embarrassment and shame are two emotions that often block sexual feelings.

Charlotte had a headache every time her husband, Paul, suggested sex. It wasn't that she had anything against sex or that she didn't enjoy sex. She knew what the problem was: She thought she was fat! She thought that to have sex with Paul would cause him to have the same feelings of disgust she had toward herself. She thought he would no longer love her or want her sexually. Charlotte had projected this fear onto her husband, and the thought of his reaction to her was so distressing that she would get a terrible, pounding headache at the very thought of sex.

In reality, Paul didn't give a fig about her weight. He did care that she was rejecting him. Once this was clear, and they were able to talk about her weight, and Paul was able to reassure her that it wasn't a problem for him, Charlotte's headaches went away. She was able to let go of her fears, and she had sex and enjoyed it. A year later when I saw them as a couple, her weight was back to normal, and the headaches were a thing of the past.

7. Someone Will Know

For many couples, sex is private. No one likes their privacy invaded, but it is particularly anxiety-provoking to think that you may be interrupted when you are having sex. Yet many couples are inhibited by such a fear all the time.

When you have children, lovemaking can be interrupted at any time. When you live with in-laws, this can put a real damper on your sex life. To let go and really have sex the way you would like is very difficult.

Tom's mother was visiting for the summer. The wall to the guest room was thin, and Lucy, Tom's wife, was uneasily aware that his mother could probably hear everything that went on. Sensing this, Lucy went through the gestures of making love, but when they had sex, she felt nothing. It was impossible for her to have an orgasm. All feeling was turned off. The thought of Tom's mother overhearing their lovemaking was a conscious mind block. Sexual feeling didn't return until Tom's mother went home.

In Lucy's case, her mother-in-law could have been given the bedroom in the basement. Or she could have been put up in a nearby motel—anything to get her out of hearing distance.

If you are worried about a child walking in, you can put a lock on the bedroom door. One reason so many parents don't do this is that they still feel guilty about having sex, guilty about even wanting privacy. There are many reasons for guilt; some have no basis but others are valid. Guilt of any kind can be a powerful mind block to sex.

What Can You Do If You Have a Mind Block About Sex?

If you have a mental block, the first step is to identify it. What is it that's causing you to feel the way you do?

Is it something you can share with your partner? If the block is something you can't share, ask yourself, "What can I do about this on my own?"

Can you put aside the memory of an old love? Or anger? Or a fantasy from the past that is interfering with your reality in the present? If not, perhaps there is an inner conflict you need help with, and perhaps you should consider seeing a therapist.

However not all mind blocks need the help of a therapist. There are many that can be resolved by sharing them with your partner. That is one of the nice things about having a partner. You have someone who is there for you and will work with you to make things better.

For example, if Sue and Jim could have talked together about the reality of the physical load she was carrying, Jim might have seen that his request for sex every night was not a reasonable request. The personal fantasy he was carrying was out of touch with the reality and causing problems in his marriage.

If you have had secret doubts about your attractiveness—a mind block that has held you back in regard to having sex—try sharing it with your partner. You may be surprised. Chances are they think you're great!

In the workshop you'll have a chance to try and identify some of these mind blocks. By listening, trying to understand, and being supportive of each other, I think you will find that many can be diminished, or even removed altogether.

The Workshop

The goal of this workshop is to identify the sexual problem or problems you may have as a couple. In the last chapter you learned that physically, through sensation, your body will respond sexually. So, all that is standing in your way is your mind! You need to put your mind to work. You need to define the sexual problem and determine how you are going to change it.

STEP #1: Define The Problem

Take five minutes each and state as briefly as possible, and as tactfully as possible, how you see the sexual problem. Write it down so you'll have a record for the future.

Listen while your partner tells you their view. Do not contradict or argue with them. If they have pointed the finger at you, do not defend yourself!

STEP #2: Working On Reality-Oriented Problems

Have you each presented a similar problem? Is it a reality problem—that is, is it something in the real world that you can identify and change? For example:

If the problem is you've each been too busy, set aside a weekend a month for vacation time together. If the problem is you are afraid of getting pregnant, make an appointment with your doctor to find out alternative ways of prevention. If the problem is your children are always there, get a babysitter regularly to take them for the evening. If the problem is that you want to have sex at different times, find and agree on a time that you both would like. Put it on your schedule and honor and keep that time.

Whatever the reality problem is, put your heads together and try to come up with a solution that is agreeable to you both.

However, what if the problem is not the same? What if you each presented two entirely different and unconnected problems?

Take a session to work on each problem individually. Solve them one by one, beginning with the one that is most critical.

What if the problem is not a reality problem—one in the real world that you can see and solve together? What if it is a problem within yourself (for example, a fear of being a failure in life, a belief you are "ugly," chronic anxiety you have trouble controlling, etc.)?

STEP #3: How To Work On Internal Problems

The first step is to identify the problem. You will need to be introspective. Ask yourself if you have feelings or thoughts that are holding you back sexually. For example: Am I too self-conscious about my body to really enjoy sex? Am I too eager to please to be able to enjoy my own pleasure? Am I angry about something and unable to talk about it? and so forth. If the problem is one you feel you can share with your partner, say, "I struggle with something that keeps me back sexually, and I would like your help to change it."

Take a few sentences and try to explain to your partner what the problem is. Then listen to what they have to say. Be willing to give your partner a chance to respond. Be willing to listen to their view and hear their suggestions, even if you don't think they will work. Be appreciative of their input, even if it doesn't contribute to solving the problem. They are trying their best.

Resolve to try to work on the problem yourself, and be ready to report on the progress you have made in the next session. Be open to considering professional help if necessary.

When it is your turn to listen to your partner's problems, be a good listener. Listen sympathetically. Let your partner tell you how they want help changing; don't give them directions or try to take control. Just be there to help.

The mind blocks we have been talking about are ones that are conscious. That is, when you think about them, you know pretty well what the problems are. Sometimes you may be aware of problems but are hard put to define them or know why they are there. You know things aren't right, but you can't put your finger on why—the reason is out of your awareness. The next chapter, "Sex and Your Unconscious," addresses such problems and will show you ways to approach them.

Chapter 10

Sex And Your Unconscious

What originally attracted you and your partner to each other? Was it sex? Did you look across the room and your eyes met? And sparks flew?

How much do you think you consciously controlled that attraction? Sure, you may have knowingly caught your partner's glance. You may have knowingly let your eyes convey that "bedroom look." But why this sudden surge of sexual interest? Where does it come from? Can you stop its flow or make it happen at will?

The factors that determine who we are and how we will act have their roots within that part of our mind that is called the "unconscious."

What is Your Unconscious?

You are your unconscious. It is that part of your mind that is out of your awareness, but it's not something separate from yourself. Within your unconscious lies all of your past; all your memories, your dreams, and your desires. From within your unconscious comes the stirring of hunger and passion that sets in motion your search for a mate. You look for a partner and, if life cooperates, you find one. However, relationships, no matter how good they are, are seldom perfect, and since sex is so highly charged emotionally, many of us come to our partner with unresolved conflicts that stem from our unconscious.

Many of such conflicts are minor and, as your relationship grows, you work them out together. But sometimes increased intimacy in itself opens old conflicts. When this is the case, the closer you and your partner become, the more difficult sex can be.

Let me give you examples of two couples who, by bringing material from the unconscious into conscious awareness, were able to resolve their sexual problems.

Ann and Mark:

Ann and Mark dated for a year before getting married. Because of religious beliefs, Ann wanted to wait until marriage before having sex. Although Mark hadn't felt the same, he'd gone along with her wishes.

Two years after their marriage, they were sitting in my office—a discouraged, angry, and unhappy couple. Ann, in a halting, embarrassed way, told me they'd never actually had intercourse. Lovemaking starts off fairly well, but at the very moment Mark tries to put his penis in, Ann has a painful vaginal spasm that makes intercourse impossible. The muscles around the vagina clamp down so that entry is impossible.

Ann told me they tried everything from playing soft music to drinking wine. She had taken tranquillizers prescribed by her family doctor and muscle relaxants prescribed by her gynecologist. She had used vaginal dilators (vaginal inserts of different sizes) to gradually stretch the vaginal opening, but nothing helped. When Mark tried to enter her vagina, the spasm returned.

Even seeing a sex therapist didn't help. Although they faithfully practiced the exercises given, when the point of actual intercourse was reached, the spasm returned.

Despite this, the therapist was still hopeful. "You need marital counseling," he said. "Then you can use what you've learned in your sessions." Seeing a marital counselor did improve their relationship. They went weekly and learned how stubborn they each were, and how to express affection, and how to compromise. But a year later the sexual problem remained unchanged. Intercourse was still impossible!

They were ready to give up. Seeing me was the last resort. "I love Ann," Mark said, "but I've really been as patient as I can. I'm tired of trying! We can't go on indefinitely like this."

I told them I couldn't promise anything, but I would certainly try to help. I asked what their lives had been like before they met. What were their families like?

Mark was the second of six children in a loving but difficult family. Although there were problems, the attitude toward sex was one of earthy acceptance. He had had two brief relationships before Ann, but Ann was the only woman he had loved and wanted to marry.

Ann, in contrast, had been an only child and the center of her mother's world until the day of the marriage. Her mother chose the food Ann would eat and the friends she had. She laid Ann's clothes out at night and helped her put them on. She worried constantly about Ann's health, even to the point of checking on her bowel movements. If Ann had not had a bowel movement by the second day, her mother would give her an enema. As Ann recounted this, her body became rigid and her voice trembled with rage.

"Ann," I asked, "do you think this is related to the sexual problem you're having?"

"The day I got married," she said, "I put it all behind me. Mother and I are finally getting along now. I don't want to feel angry with her again. I don't want to remember how it was."

Ann had pushed the struggle with her mother into her unconscious. There it was hidden but not gone. Her earlier need to defend herself against an invasion of her body was being expressed now by the vaginal spasm. Until Ann could consciously separate the two events (the dreaded enemas of the past and the desired intercourse of the present), her body would continue to go into spasm and prevent what she most desired: sex with Mark.

In the session Ann recalled the dreaded experience of the enemas. She saw the connection between the spasm caused by the enemas and the spasm occurring inappropriately with Mark. Once the mind sees something, it can no longer be blind. When Ann realized the connection (in psychoanalytic terms, "had insight"), the tie was broken. She and Mark were able to have sex and enjoy it, and now, some years later, they have a successful relationship and two handsome sons.

This may seem a rather extreme example, but many women have unconscious fears that block their sexuality. Many women have experienced sexual abuse, have had a distant or ambivalent relationship with their father, or have had a mother who forbade sexuality. Such memories, long put aside and buried within the unconscious, can block the normal flow of sexual feelings.

Of course, not only women have such unconscious blocks. Men, too, have buried fears that can interfere with sexual desire, and uncovering such fears can go a long way toward resolving them.

Tony and Marianne:

Tony had had sex with many women, but Marianne was the first woman he had fallen in love with. She was special. In fact, he wanted to marry her. In contrast to the other women Tony had known, he really "respected" Marianne, and he had not pushed to have sex before marriage.

To his shock, on their wedding night he was impotent. For the first time, he failed to get an erection. Absolutely nothing happened!

Marianne had been very understanding, but Tony was totally unnerved. This had never happened to him before. What did it mean?

Marianne was patient and understanding and, a few days later, having put the episode behind them, Mark attempted to make love to her again. Again, nothing happened. Again, he was impotent!

Looking very anxious, he came to see me the following day. I asked if he had any thoughts as to why he would have a problem. "No," he said, "this has never happened before." He wanted to know why it should happen now with the one person he felt he truly cared for. It was totally frustrating!

Tony had a problem common to many men. He had what is called a "Madonna/whore" complex. Tony thought that with nice girls, ones you "really" love, you don't have sex. Oh, he didn't think this consciously, but his conviction was so strong that he lost his erection each time he tried to make love with Marianne.

In the session, Tony told me how sex had always been regarded as a dirty joke in his family. It was his father who told the jokes, but never when his mother was there. Although Tony knew differently, he would have said his mother was above having sex. Never, never would she enjoy it or do it!

Like a little kid, Tony thought it wasn't any more okay to have sex with Marianne than it would be to have sex with Mother. Before he could maintain an erection, he had to get rid of the notion that nice people, people you love, don't have sex!

In order to solve his problem, Tony, like Ann, had to bring it to light. As Tony recalled his feelings, I pointed out to him how these inappropriate childhood impressions had been carried forward into adulthood. Tony could then see that he had displaced these same feelings about his mother onto Marianne. Once the distinction was clear in his mind, sex ceased to be a problem.

You may wonder: Is it possible to remove such barriers without the help of a therapist? Is it even wise to try?

Can you be your own therapist?

Being Your Own Therapist

Yes, you can be your own therapist! Some problems may need the help of a professional, but many you can work on and change by yourself.

You can't force your way into your unconscious. That only makes the barriers more powerful. However, if you are cagey, you can catch glimpses here and there as to its contents.

According to Freud, dreams are the royal path to the unconscious. And, indeed, they are. If you have a dream, write it down before it slips away. Then read it and see what comes to mind. Did the dream express a fear, a wish, a hope? Did you learn anything about yourself?

What about slips of the tongue?

When a word pops out to replace another it reveals an unconscious association. An example I can give is a personal one that amuses me. When I call my daughter, to my surprise out comes my younger sister's name! It is clear that in my unconscious I see my daughter as my younger sister.

In addition to slips of the tongue, another clue to the unconscious is that the emotional response you have to a situation is way out of bounds. You are excessively sensitive, excessively anxious, unusually reactive. Often your partner is more aware when this happens than you are. They've probably been burned more than once by reactions they don't understand.

Let me give you the example of Mary and Tim:

Mary and Tim were about to make love when the phone rang next to their bed. Mary reached over and picked it up. It was her son calling long-distance, and she chatted a moment or two before saying, "Can I call you back tomorrow? We've just gone to bed." She hung up, rolled over, and put her arms around her husband.

He pushed her away. "What's wrong?" she asked. "Nothing," he said, "I've just lost interest." He moved to the edge of the bed, and for several days following he was distant and cold to her.

Perhaps Mary shouldn't have answered the phone at that moment. However, Tim's reaction was clearly an overreaction. Tim didn't know why he was so upset. If asked, he would have denied any jealousy toward Mary's son.

Is it possible for them to work on this together? Yes, it is. Mary can say, "You know, perhaps that was a bad time to pick up the phone, but I really think you over-reacted. How come?"

If Tim can allow himself to be introspective and find out why he was so upset, then they have a chance to set the problem right. If Tim can share with Mary the feelings he does indeed have about her son, then they have a place to begin. They will understand each other better, and there may be things they can do in reality that will help. For example, they can agree that the phone doesn't get answered when they are about to make love.

I've had many instances in which, when asked to think about questions between sessions, patients have returned with answers they've found themselves. These were answers they didn't know they had. Let me give you a couple of examples:

Eileen and Sam:

Eileen brought Sam to therapy because he had lost interest in her sexually. Eileen was a beautiful young woman who couldn't understand why this had happened, and Sam was unable to explain it as well.

Parents of an eighteen-month-old baby girl, they had had no difficulty sexually before her birth. Why now? In the session, Sam was cooperative, but every idea as to why his interest in sex had disappeared led nowhere. He just "wasn't interested."

"Well," I said, "give yourself a chance to think about it. See if you can't put your finger on what it might be before you come for the next session."

When Sam walked in the next time, he looked very pleased with himself. "I know exactly what the problem is," he said. "I'm afraid Eileen will get pregnant again. We simply can't afford another baby. Not financially or emotionally. Much as I love our little daughter, she wasn't planned. I think Eileen wants another baby, and I'm scared it's going to happen. No way can I enjoy sex, not until I know for sure we're in agreement about this."

Sarah:

Another example of a patient who found her own answer is Sarah. Sarah prided herself on not getting angry. She was quite surprised to find the answer was that she was indeed quite angry with her boyfriend. It's not at all uncommon to discover that the enjoyment of sex is being blocked by anger pushed out of awareness.

Sarah walks every morning, and she told me that in this time her mind solves problems, remembers dreams, and contemplates relationships. "My mind floats on its own," she said. "Sometimes I don't even see the world around me."

Sarah had been having a lot of difficulty with her boyfriend. She recently had come to me to understand why she missed him terribly when he was away, but when he came home she lost all interest in sex. We had talked about it in the session, but she had no idea why this should happen. "Why don't you think about it on your walk?" I asked. "See what comes to mind."

Sure enough, at the next session, Sarah said, "I know exactly what's wrong. I'm furious with him for going away. He can just come and go, and I'm the one left behind. Then he walks back into my life and, with a snap of his fingers, expects me to be intimate with him!"

These are examples of couples who were able to work on unconscious psychic blocks on their own. They brought the problem to light, worked on it, then made it go away. This isn't always possible. Sometimes, professional help is needed. Whether or not you can deal with the problem often depends on the support you can give each other. Bringing a warm and loving attitude to the session is critical, and that is the first step in the workshop.

The Workshop

STEP #1: Setting The Stage

Say to your partner, "I love you and I want to come closer to you. I think we may each be bringing hang-ups that are getting in the way of how we want our sex life to be. Maybe we aren't even aware of them. I want to change that as much as I can."

STEP #2: Bringing The Problem To Light

Since sometimes excessive emotional response is a clue to an unconscious conflict, ask your partner, "Do you think I'm oversensitive in some way about sex? Do you think I overreact at times?"

Try to listen to their answer without becoming defensive or hurt. Try to understand their point of view.

As with any problem, you will need to decide if this is an issue you can work on together, or if you will need the help of a therapist.

STEP #3: Is This A Problem We Can Work On?

Unconscious problems are complex. Sometimes they tap into feelings and areas of the mind that need professional help.

If you are dissatisfied with the workshop, or feel you have gotten in over your head, don't try to push the limits beyond what you are comfortable with. Instead, ask your partner, "Do you think we can deal with this on our own or should we get counseling?"

If you feel the problem is too difficult, tell your partner honestly, "I'm sorry, but this is too sensitive an area for me. I would feel more comfortable if we could talk to a therapist."

On the other hand, if you both feel the problem is something you can work on, forge ahead!

STEP #4: *Working On The Problem*

Sometimes just talking about a problem is helpful.

Sometimes just knowing about the roots of a problem can help resolve it, for once the conscious mind sees something clearly it cannot go back to the old state of being "unaware."

And sometimes just being given loving support, and being listened to, is enough to begin a healing process.

STEP #5: *Schedule Another Session*

The purpose of this first session on unconscious factors was just to open the door a little. Give yourselves time to think over what was said, and schedule another session in about a week's time.

Don't try to solve all the problems at once. Sometimes just being able to talk about a problem area and getting your partner's support is enough to reduce the problem without doing any more about it. Sometimes solving one problem is like starting a block of dominos; once begun, they all fall into line.

However, don't have unrealistic expectations. A lot depends on the seriousness and depth of the problem. A lot depends on you and you your partner, and your strength and capacity to tolerate stress and respond sympathetically to each other.

Don't push or rush the process; if you have identified a possible problem, give yourselves time to think about it. Schedule another session in a week and use the time between to be self-reflective. Think about what your partner has said, see if it rings true, and, if so, bring thoughts to the session as to how to begin change. A realistic goal is to reduce anxiety so sex becomes the pleasure it should be.

Part III

Couples And Family

Chapter 11

Couples And Children

How about Children?

Almost all couples will face the question, "How about children?" For some, the answer will come easily; for others, the choice may be much more difficult. The goal of this chapter is to help provide a safe place where each of you can talk openly about your feelings in regard to having children.

Fifty years ago, the choice whether to have children or not was very limited. Prior to the advent of birth control, babies either came or they didn't. It was considered God's will. We didn't have the agonizing, indescribably heavy responsibility of deciding whether or not to bring a child into this world.

Now, however, birth control provides a way other than abstinence to prevent conception. And, for the first time in history, if conception does not occur, medical science offers options never dreamed of before. Today's couples face decisions about having children that are more complex and difficult than at any time in the past.

The first questions are individual ones. You need to ask yourself: Do I want children? How important is this to me? Is it a wish I can set aside, or is it something in life I must have?

Perhaps you don't know the answer to this question yet. Perhaps the answer needs to come later in your life and will depend on the wishes of your partner, your financial situation, or other variables.

However, if you know the answer now, it is important that you let your partner know. Keeping silent, or holding back this knowledge, is like a canker sore lying at the core of your relationship. It is not fair to you or to your partner.

Sometimes people know but carefully hide their feelings. They may be afraid to bring up the subject for fear it is premature. Or they may be afraid that if they let their feelings be known, the relationship will end.

I have seen long-term relationships seriously jeopardized because the partners have been unable to share their real feelings as to having children.

Such secrets cause much damage. It is really so much easier and so much better in the long run to be able to state clearly at the onset of the relationship what your feelings are. The easiest way is to lay your cards on the table right away, to be able to state outright how you feel about having a family. Don't be afraid to put it on the line: "One thing I know about myself is that I really don't want children," or "One thing I know is that someday I am really looking forward to having a family," or, "You know, I'm not sure yet how I feel about having children."

Such a statement could perhaps end the relationship right then and there. But isn't it better to know now rather than several years hence (just as it's better to know a person's intent as to commitment)? If a partner has no intent on marrying, it is only fair to make this clear. Or, if a partner has no intent on having children, again it is only fair to make this clear early on, before feelings are deeply involved.

Although it is advisable to find out the other person's wishes about children early in a relationship, in reality many couples leave the decision until later on. Then it may be more difficult to bring the subject up. You may be hesitant about putting pressure on your partner. You may question whether your commitment to each other is really that strong and wonder if this is the right time. You may be fearful of treading on sensitive ground—not being able to have children can carry a deep implication of failure.

Difficult as talking about this is, however, it is preferable to silence. I am reminded of a young woman I saw for chronic depression. In the course of taking her history, I found out that she was unable to have children. Although her husband had reassured her years ago that this was not a problem for him, she was convinced that he was secretly disappointed. This important subject had been mentioned once and then not brought up again. For her, the silence had covered painful feelings that eventually led to depression.

The Pros and Cons of Having Children

There is nothing more wonderful than having a child. It is a life experience unmatched!

However, it is not for everyone, and if your decision is that it is not for you, that's fine. There are already too many people in this world! You are doing the world a favor.

For those who desire a child, as wonderful as this is, they need to answer these questions: Do you understand the choice you are making? Are you prepared for the changes ahead? Do you know that your lifestyle as a couple will be disrupted? Are you prepared for the sacrifices you will have to make?

The questions are many, the choices often difficult. Different individuals have different concerns. Some may worry about economic stability. Women worry about their age and how to combine having children with their life career. As time goes on, however, the situation may change and feelings may change. If you are comfortable talking to each other, you can take these changes in stride. Talking openly about these feelings is far better than keeping quiet.

Today, medical science offers a variety of choices in regard to having children. Not being able to conceive, or having difficulty conceiving, or being in a same sex relationship are no longer the end of the road. There is now a whole range of options open to you.

Questions you need to ask yourself are: How far are you willing to go in the pursuit of parenthood? Do you want to go to a fertility clinic? It is not just that some of these procedures involve immense amounts of money, but there is an emotional price to pay as well. Trying to conceive is an immense strain on a couple. It shifts what should be a shared, intimate, and personal experience to a public test of performance.

And if, after all the effort, conception does not occur, there will be the final question: "Do we want to adopt?" Where there are differences of feeling, this can be a most sensitive area.

Certainly, the closer you are to agreement on the issues around having children, the easier making decisions will be. However, decisions of this magnitude warrant more than a simple agreement. If feelings are buried, they can cause great problems and resentment later. The impact can have repercussions on all aspects of the relationship.

The following workshop is intended to present a framework in which you can open up and share feelings with each other. To be successful, the environment must be accepting and noncritical. Try to allow this to happen by being supportive of your partner. Try to be willing to compromise where there are differences.

This chapter cannot help you make the decision as to having children—that must come from within yourselves—but it can help you talk about it.

Workshop Assignment

There is a preassignment for this workshop; prior to coming, write a brief paragraph about your own childhood experience. Was it pleasant? Was it unhappy? Did you like being a child?

Then write a paragraph on what your feelings are now as to having children. Be as honest as you can. Don't be afraid of saying, "No, this is not for me" because you think only bad people would say no. Don't be afraid to say, "Yes, I really would like to have children" for fear it will put a burden on your partner. Don't be fearful of acknowledging uncertainty; uncertainty is the normal and natural state before you have enough data to make a decision.

The Workshop

STEP #1: Read Aloud The Paragraph You Wrote As To What It Was Like To Be A Child

This is important because your view of what you would like the environment to be for your child, or what you would want it not to be, is strongly influenced by the experiences you had as a child.

STEP #2: Read Aloud The Paragraph You Wrote As To How You Feel About Having Children

Realize as you read the paragraph that you are expressing only your current feelings. You can never really predict how you will actually feel when and if you have a child. Nor can you predict, for sure, how you will feel years hence if you make a decision not to have a child. Some of the most fearful and apprehensive people have, when the time comes, turned into the most dedicated and devoted parents. The statement you make is not meant to box you in. Feelings are not fixed in time; they depend on many variables. You may change—people do.

STEP #3: What Are The Differences Between You In Regard To Having Children

How serious are these differences? Is compromise possible? Can you work to reach a compromise?

Do you want two children or four? Does one of you feel confident about parenting and the other insecure and anxious? Do you want children right now, or would you prefer to wait four or five years? There are many areas in which compromise and an attitude of mutual support can make solutions possible.

The degree to which each person can compromise will be related to the intensity of their feelings and such factors as career plans, the status of their health, their age, their financial goals, and so forth. In the process of compromise, there is a limit beyond which it is not possible to go. Each person needs to find that limit and let their partner know.

STEP #4: *Secret Wishes*

If you have buried certain hopes or wishes in regard to children, shouldn't you give your partner a chance to hear them?

To try to trick your partner or to anticipate that they will change is unfair, and it usually does not work. I saw one couple in which the woman had tricked the man, knowing he did not want children. The child, now a girl of fourteen, had been hated and resented by her father. The relationship of the mother and father had become increasingly bitter. It was a sad story.

Don't be ashamed of feelings. You have a right to your feelings. Respect them and your partner's as well. Consider individual therapy for one or both of you if you think this would be helpful. If it turns out that you are truly incompatible in this regard, the relationship may not be right for either one of you.

However, leave the door open to future discussions.

Sometimes people say nothing because they think it will do no good to speak up. Nothing will change. That may be so; nevertheless, talking and understanding can change feelings. If one is appreciated for the sacrifice one is making—for what one is giving up—it can make a big difference. Silently burying wishes, or giving up hopes, stops the normal process of coming to terms with the loss. On the other hand, being able to talk about a loss in a way that is met with understanding can allow integration of the loss. Then one can move on and participate in the relationship fully and without rancor.

Chapter 12

Couples And Family

If it is difficult being a couple, it is even more difficult being a family. Whereas two is a perfect number for relating, three, by its very nature, is a difficult one. Someone is always on the outside, for only two people can make contact at once.

As a couple, there are just the two of you, but, when the first baby arrives, it is Mother (or the stay-at-home partner) and baby that become the twosome. Father (or the partner working outside the home) is number three. What can happen in the transition from couple to family is that the "couple" relationship is lost.

When baby gets old enough to take the first steps and reaches out to Father suddenly it is Mother (or the stay-at-home partner) who momentarily becomes the outsider.

Thus begins the interactions of all families: the jealousies, the competition, and the struggles for closeness and love.

Later, there may be more children. Although this may help balance things a little—now there are two and two rather than two and one—it also further complicates things. Each new baby is a stranger who has to work their way into the family. The first child is shifted from center position to the sidelines. The new baby struggles to find his or her place. Each child would like most of all to come up and stay in that wonderful territory belonging to the parents, the "couple" territory.

When I was a psychiatric resident, I was privileged to be able to go to Salvador Minuchin's Family Clinic in Philadelphia for two weeks. What a two weeks!

As we, the students, watched from the sidelines, Dr. Minuchin demonstrated the principles of his structural family therapy and how he worked with families. I remember, in particular, a large family of perhaps twelve people whom he had sit in a circle. Then he went from one family member to the next, welcoming each in turn. When he came to a small child, he would drop down to the child's level and look into their eyes as he shook their hands. He charmed everyone.

The structural principles he presented are ones I took away with me and have used ever since. I would like to share them with you, for if you understand the structure of a healthy family, you can work to create one for yourself. A family becomes troubled when the parents are divided. If your territory as a couple is eroded—that is, if the space between the two of you has been invaded—you need to reclaim it. If your boundaries as a couple have been destroyed, you need to reestablish them. Be it in-laws, or children, or some outside force, your first loyalty needs to be to each other.

Splitting in a Family

The word commonly used to describe the process of children coming between parents is "splitting." A certain amount of splitting in a family is to be expected and is quite normal. But for a couple whose relationship is already troubled, the addition of a child can further divide the family into opposing forces. The child can become a vehicle that is used as an ally by one parent against the other. The family can become divided against itself.

Happy families tend to have a similar splitting pattern; the split is horizontal between generations. On the contrary, in unhappy families, splitting occurs vertically, dividing the parents and separating some family members from others.

By drawing circles to represent family members, you can make a picture of your own family. Let me show you some examples (though these diagrams depict a more traditional model of a family structure, you can draw them in whatever way suits your own family):

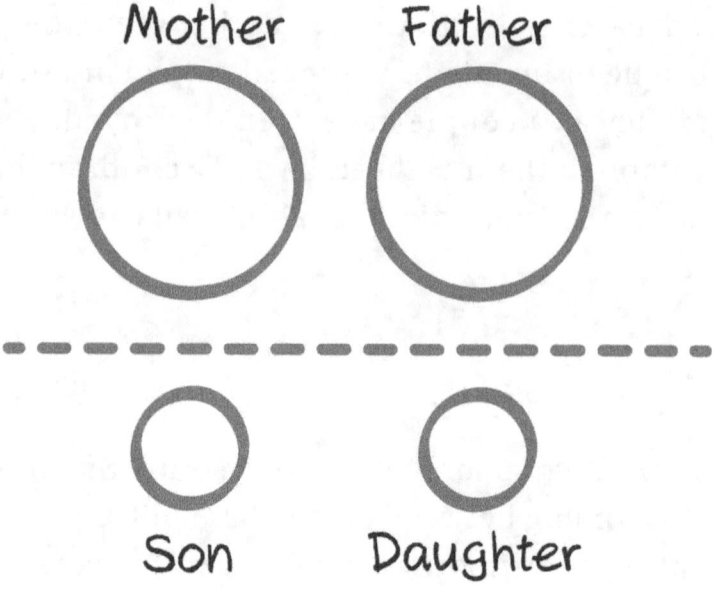

Figure #1: A Drawing of a Happy Family

In the example above, the split in the family is indicated by the dotted line. It is horizontal, lying between the two generations. The parents have their own territory and their children have theirs.

In the next example, the illustration is of the same family, but the split is vertical. You can see that it divides the family, separating the parents. This is a recipe for an unhappy family.

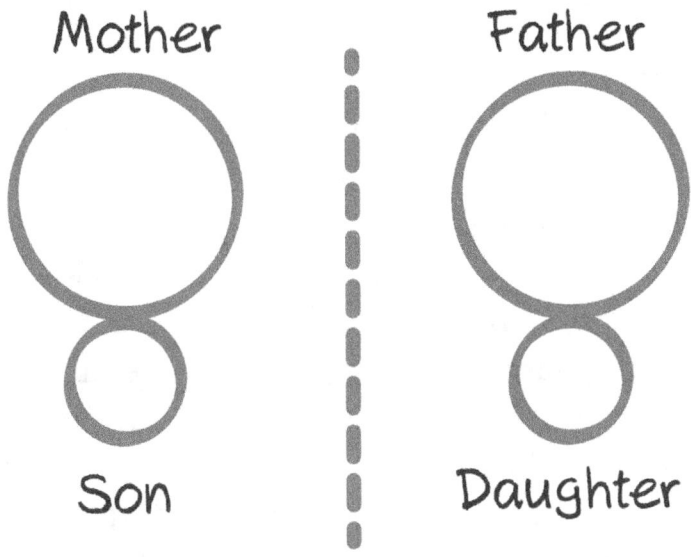

Figure #2: A Drawing of an Unhappy Family

Here, the mother is closest to the son, and the father is closest to the daughter. The family is divided right down the middle. The task is to realign the family so that the parents are together in their own territory, and the children are placed in a territory that is theirs.

The mother has to be willing to relinquish some of the closeness with her son, encouraging his relationship to his father. And, similarly, the father has to give up some of his closeness to his daughter, encouraging her to have a closer relationship with her mother.

Such changes are not easy but are well worth the effort. The children, in particular, will cling to the old patterns. Change takes patience and the willingness to keep trying on the part of both parents.

Power in a Family

In addition to the splitting process described above, the power balance in a family is very important.

What is power? It is the right to participate in decision making. It is the right to be regarded with respect. It is the right to be listened to when you speak. It is the right to be important.

In a healthy family, although the children have some power, the parents should be in charge. However, a surprising number of parents are hesitant to take the power they should have. Perhaps they are afraid of hurting a child, yet too much power is as destructive for the child as it is difficult for the parents. A child given too much power, too early, can suffer their entire life from an impaired sense of reality. A child given too much power, too early, is deprived of childhood. And when children have inappropriate power, the parents are deprived of a life of their own.

Ideally, the distribution of power between partners should be equal. In the very recent past, however, this was not so. The man was the dominant figure, and as the head of the family he was supposed to hold the power. If this was not so, he was looked on as being weak, even considered a failure within his own family.

The dramatic change in the status of women has altered this somewhat. Since the strings of power are often attached to money, the fact that women are now more equal wage-earners can be both a blessing and a curse—for this is a change that can be threatening to many men.

Being able to talk about this openly is better than keeping it hidden. The workshop that follows gives you the opportunity to diagram and look at your family's structure, and also allows you to show the distribution of power by the size of the circles you draw.

Before starting the workshop, it is recommended that you look it over to see if it is appropriate for your family. If your family's problems are too severe, such as incest, alcohol or drug abuse, or mental illness, professional help should come first. You can always return to this workshop later.

The Workshop

STEP #1: Your Family Structure

Each partner should draw a picture of the family structure. Designate each family member by a circle. Draw the circles on a sheet of paper with their positions indicating their closeness to the other members. If the parents are very close, draw them as two circles touching. They are at the top of the drawing. Beneath them place the circles indicating the children.

If one child is closer to Mother (or the stay-at-home partner) than to Father (or the other partner), place the child's circle closer to Mother. If one child is so close to Mother that the child separates the parents, place the circle right next to Mother and move Father across the page.

Draw a dotted line to show how the family is divided. Ideally, the line should run horizontally, dividing one generation from the next. When children have come between the parents, the family will be split into two separate sides, and the line will run vertically.

STEP #2: Compare The Drawings You Have Made Of Your Family

Are they similar? Talk about the differences. Why might it be that you see things differently? Explain to each other your reasons for placing the circles the way you have.

STEP #3: Identify Family Problems On The Basis Of The "Splitting" In The Diagrams

Is there a separation of generations? Is the split between generations horizontal, or does the split pass through vertically, separating the family into two camps?

Has the family been divided into groups with some members allied on one side against those on the other side? Is one family member way out on the periphery?

STEP #4: Power Balances In The Family

Make the size of the circles correspond to the power that each person has in the family. Using the same diagrams as you did for the structure of the family, adjust the size of the circles to correspond to the distribution of power in the family.

STEP #5: Identify Family Problems On The Basis Of Inappropriate Power Distribution

Do you see a problem? Is the power balance between the parents fair? What about the children? Does one child have more power than another? Is the power distribution appropriate to the ages of the children?

STEP #6: Realignment Of Splitting

Plan how to realign the splitting in a way that brings your family structure closer to that of the happy family.

For example, if you, as a couple, have been divided by the children, resolve to stand together and support each other. If you, individually, have had favorites or allies, Resolve to shift and bring about a better alignment within the family. Work to make the natural division between generations rather than between family members.

STEP #7: Plan How To Redistribute Power In A More Balanced Way

If one member of the family has had too much power, the family needs to talk and plan how to rebalance this. In a healthy family the power is shared equally between the two parents. Too much power given to a child is destructive to both child and parents. Too much power given to the parents leads to either intimidated, fearful children or angry, rebellious children. The correct balance of power is difficult to achieve but is always worth striving for.

Chapter 13

The "Problem" Child

Childhood is not easy; most children at some time in their lives will have a problem. Parenting is not easy, and most parents at some time will have a problem with a child. Do you have a "problem" child?

The Child's View

We forget how it was to be a child. For the most part, however, we didn't feel like "a child." We were just who we were, trying to get along the best we could in a world not of our making. The view of us as a child was in other people's eyes. If you talk to adults about their childhood, what they remember most clearly is often an experience as a child of trying to do something right and instead making a terrible mistake, which upset the adults to no end!

No doubt you can give your own example of good intentions gone astray, but the most recent one I heard was of a little girl trying to please Mommy by bringing her breakfast in bed. The problem was she used the Limoges china and Mother became hysterical. What a "bad" child she was!

Fifty years later, this "child" related the episode to me with tears in her eyes.

If you have been seeing your son or daughter as a "bad" child, I can almost guarantee that things will get better when you view this child differently. Children get caught in being "bad" and they don't know how to find their way out. Seeing the problem as something separate from your child can make a world of difference.

The goal is to become the child's ally, to take the child's side and find out what is wrong.

A Different Light

When a child has a problem or becomes a problem, he or she becomes the center of focus. The task would seem to be to "fix" the child. This may be appropriate in some cases: the child needs medical attention, the child needs tutoring, the child needs discipline, and so forth. But there is another way of seeing the problem, and that is that the child is caught up in a situation, and it is the situation that is the problem, not the child.

In the previous chapter, "Couples and Family," it was shown how diagramming the family structure could be a useful adjunct to understanding problems. The same is true in regard to children; understanding a child's position in the family can be a useful tool for understanding why he or she is having a problem.

The focus in this chapter will be on the family structure with particular attention to the problem child. You will be able to see some answers to these questions: Is this child left out? Isolated? Closer to one parent or the other? Does the child have too much power? Has the child intimidated everyone by his or her "bad" behavior? Is the child seen as the "bad one," the troublemaker, the one who is always going to screw up?

The diagrams of two family structures below illustrate how they can not only bring problems to light but can also open up a way to correct them.

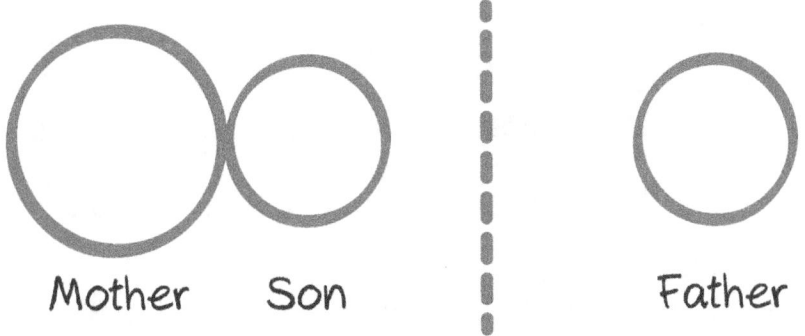

Figure #3: Problem Family with Mother and Son on One Side and Father on the Other

In the diagram above, you see that the child is overly close to Mother and overly powerful in the family. Father has been pushed far to the outer borders. This is good for no one.

What needs to change?

Mother needs to relinquish the excessive closeness to her son and come closer to the father. Father needs to move back into the picture and be more active in parenting. Mother and Father need to reestablish their closeness.

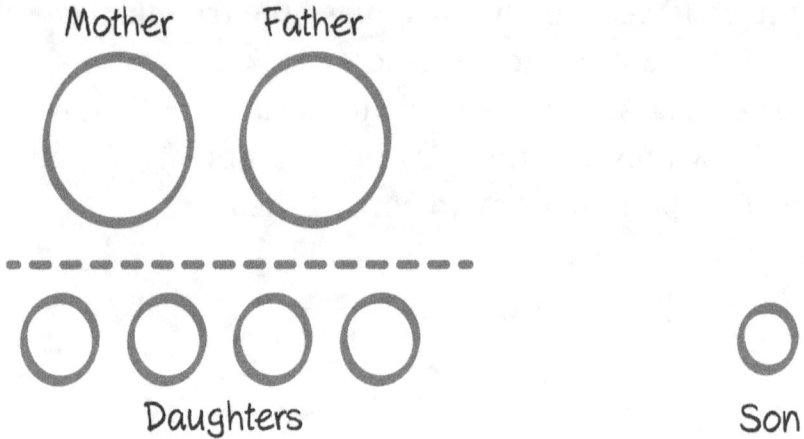

Figure #4: A Family with a Problem Son

Mother and Father are close, and the four little sisters are close, but the one boy is far out on the periphery. He is seen as the naughty, bad boy who is rude and clumsy and somewhat stupid. All his sisters excel in school, but he doesn't do his homework, plays hooky, and is often sullen and rebellious.

What is the problem here?

We don't know by just looking at the diagram: perhaps Father has been too busy to give his son male support in this family of girls, perhaps Mother doesn't understand boys, perhaps this son has a problem with school that has made him feel a failure. But what we do know from the diagram is that he has been excluded from the family circle and that he must feel very isolated and alone. He must feel like a "bad" person.

One of the tasks is to bring the son back into the family, to make him feel accepted. This will take a conscious effort on the part of the parents. To be successful, it will require a change in attitude toward him. It will require letting go of seeing him as the "bad" child—and seeing him instead as a child who needs help.

The workshop that follows provides an opportunity to look at your own family structure. As a couple, you will share your observations with the hope of gaining greater understanding not only of your child but of the entire family.

The Workshop

STEP #1: Consider Your Roles As Parents

Discuss the feelings you have toward your child.

Ask yourself: What kind of a parent am I? Am I a perfectionist? Do I have a favorite in the family? Have I set a good example?

Do you feel angry at the child?

If so, try to let these feelings go. Think instead: Something is wrong, but this is not a bad child. Something is causing this behavior, and our task is to find out the problem.

If you feel your partner is at fault, let these feelings go also. The point of the session is not to place blame; it is to resolve the problem. If you cannot work together and be supportive of each other, you will not be able to help your child. Resolve to listen to what your partner has to say. Resolve to let defensiveness go.

STEP #2: Identify Major Problems That May Be Outside Of The Family Structure

Share thoughts you have on this subject. Is this child failing in school? Does this child have a health problem? Does he or she have friends? What about drug or alcohol use?

Understand that this workshop is going to focus on your child within the family structure and that other issues will momentarily be set aside.

STEP #3: Each Of You Diagram The Family Structure As You See It With Particular Attention To This Child (Refer To Chapter 12, "Couples And Family," As To How To Diagram A Family)

When finished, compare the diagrams. Where is the child located in the family structure? Are there problems with closeness? Are there problems with power? Do you know how to change the structure in a way that will improve things for the child?

Do your diagrams differ? If so, how? Can you reconcile the differences?

STEP #4: Each Of You Write Down A Brief Description Of How You See The Structural Problem And What Can Be Done

Punishment has no place in dealing with a child in trouble. Children naturally want to please, want to be loved, want to be good. If this is not the case, an underlying problem has not been identified. Punishment in these circumstances will only breed feelings of hatred, resentment, and a wish for revenge—just the opposite of what you are trying to achieve.

Step #5: Share Your Views And Formulate A Joint Plan Of Action

Ask, "How have we contributed to the problem?"

Do not blame each other. Be supportive. Discuss whether you feel you can work with the problem yourselves. Is your relationship as a couple stable enough? What risks are there? Is there a risk to the child?

Remember, getting professional help if necessary is not a sign of weakness but of strength.

STEP #6: Should Children Be Included In The Planning?

If it is a very young child—no. The parents need to be in total control. For example, suppose a three-year-old demands to sleep in the parents' bed. The child has temper tantrums when put in his or her own bed. Both parents must agree ahead of time on how to manage this. It is appropriate to tell the child that it is time to sleep in their own bed; it is not appropriate to ask the child their opinion.

The parents need to stand together. One parent must not then give in and go and bring the child back into their bed. On the other hand, if the plan is not working, if it seems too abrupt for the child to handle, both parents, together, must be agreeable to altering it. They don't make the change because the child is demanding it; they make the change because they feel it is in the best interest of the child.

Including Older Children

When possible, older children should be included in the plan. They can even help in drawing the family structure. Where do they feel they fit in the family? Where would they like to be?

The "problem" adolescent can be particularly difficult. However, when parents' attitudes change and adolescents are listened to with respect and understanding, dramatic changes can occur.

An example is Kathy, who is fourteen and refuses to keep her room neat. Up until recently she has kept her room fairly orderly, but now she defiantly refuses. Her attitude is bad. Food is left under the bed, trash accumulates, and dirty clothes are thrown on the floor.

What could be the problem?

Drawing the family structure reveals a pretty normal, healthy family with the three children (Kathy is the middle of three sisters) in their own territory and the parents in theirs.

But what does stand out is that her older sister has just left for college and many of her duties have now fallen to Kathy.

Could this be part of the problem? Is Kathy feeling unjustly put-upon? Envious of her sister's achievement? Or, is she missing her sister? Perhaps feeling left behind?

Kathy and her family drew the family structure together. The diagram showed that now only the two younger sisters were at home. Kathy talked about how much she missed her older sister, and also the fact that her responsibilities were heavier and she didn't think that was fair.

Did her room improve?

A little.

What was really important, however, was that her attitude changed. She was, once again, the good-natured Kathy that she had always been.

The above examples deal with fairly minor problems. In reality, the best-intentioned plans sometimes do not work. You have to be willing to alter your plan, possibly even to alter your view of what the problem is.

Try to be patient. The path is not easy, but the rewards can be great.

Chapter 14

Couples With Stepchildren

Couples and stepchildren often mix like oil and water—only with great difficulty. If you have read Chapter 11, you have read how children compound rather than simplify a relationship. The same can be said for stepchildren, but many times over.

Instead of two parents in roles of authority, there are four. Instead of two sets of grandparents, there may be as many as four or more.

To make matters worse, a good proportion of the children and adults are struggling with hurt and anger from the past. Feelings are fragile and emotions are easily triggered.

Although most of the adults, most of the time, are well-intentioned and want to do the best they can, it is not easy. The situation is like a battlefield, studded with emotional explosives that can go off at any time. Hard-won truces hang delicately in balance. New relationships try bravely, against all odds, to move ahead into positions of strength.

The situation can be a nightmare for the children as well as the adults. Usually, the children aren't babies. They come to the new relationship with well-developed personalities, most often complicated by the painful feelings that go hand in hand with the break up of families.

Almost always, there is not enough money. The children struggle for survival, and in the process they alienate and divide parents and stepparents. Parents, desperately trying to do the right thing, are often overwhelmed.

Small wonder that stress is intense. In many cases, it can be so intense that the fragile, new structure of the family collapses. The children are left again to face another disruptive change. Feelings of both adults and children run the gamut from abandonment and loss to possible triumph contaminated with guilt.

Does the above picture fit you at all? If so, have heart; it is not hopeless. Although the problems are not ones that will go away overnight, a great deal can be done to help families get on the right track.

Can you do it without professional help? That, you will have to assess—but why not give it a try? See how the workshop goes. If it is not enough, take the step: get counseling. For it is not just your relationship as a couple that is at stake; it is the fate of your entire family.

Preparation for the Workshop

As usual, your emotional state can have a direct bearing on how the session goes. Two factors are important: One, how committed are you to the relationship? Two, how mature are you prepared to be?

Your Commitment to the Relationship

What happens to your family depends upon your ability to work together as a couple. Before beginning the session, you need to clarify, in your own mind, your position in the relationship. Are you on the verge of giving up? Or, indeed, have you already given up and agreed to the session only as a final "gesture"? If so, now is the time to reconsider.

Ask yourself: Am I willing to fight for this family? Am I willing to undergo the sacrifices it may take? The answers to these questions can only come from within yourself. The answers are crucial to the work that lies ahead.

Maturity

The next question you need to ask of yourself is, How mature am I? People are often older in second relationships, but, unfortunately, not always more mature. Some people seem to be born mature; other people act like children until the day they die.

What does it mean to be "mature"? It means the capacity to, at times, put others ahead of yourself. It means accepting the fact that you can't control the world, or even those close to you. In terms of having stepchildren, it means that you can tolerate others, that you can tolerate not always being "the center," and that you can let go of judging others by your own standards of perfection.

Can maturity be learned? Yes. What it demands is, first, that you see it is necessary and want to work toward it, and, second, that you see it is ultimately rewarding in ways that are very important to you.

Family Structure Diagram

In preparation for the workshop to follow, each of you diagram the structure of your family and associated previous family members. Refer to Chapter 12 as a guide to do this. In the center of the diagram, place your present family, including stepchildren. Off to the side, place previous family members who still impact your life. As in Chapter 12, use circles to designate different family members. Make the size of the circles proportionate to their power within the family structure.

The principles of a healthy family remain the same. Ideally, there needs to be a horizontal split between generations, not a vertical split separating the family into conflicting sides. The couple must be together in their own territorial space. Within this space they make joint decisions.

Such a space is not easily maintained in a family complicated by stepchildren. Children, by their very nature, want to get close to their parents and claim them as their very own. This need may be even stronger for a stepchild. It takes loving strength, therefore, on the part of the parents to not allow children, whether natural or step-, to come between them and alienate and divide them.

Compare the drawing of your family as it is now with a second drawing to show how you would like it to be. Reality will dictate much of what you draw; for example, a stepchild may only visit on certain holidays, so the drawings have to take that into account. However, even then the stepchild should not invade the territory of the parents or have too much power.

Below is an illustration of what a family structure with a stepchild might look like at the beginning of the relationship. Then there is a second drawing to show how certain needed changes were made.

Figure #5: Family with a Stepchild in the Beginning

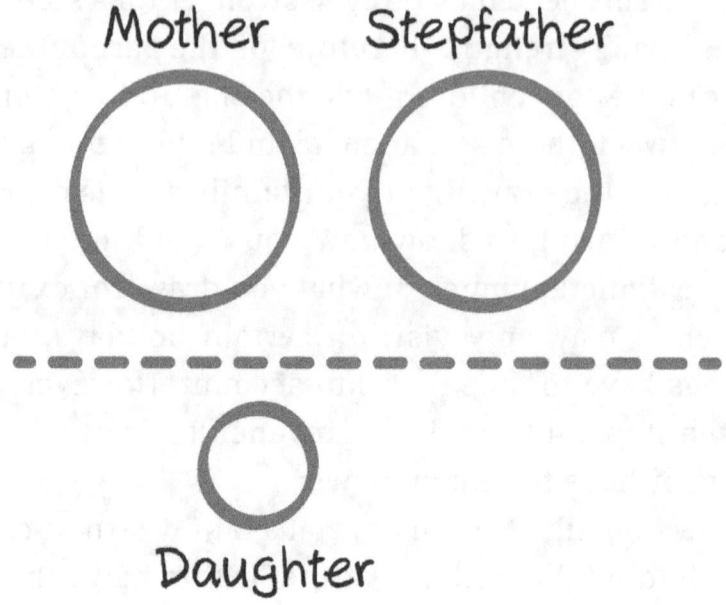

Figure #6: Family with a Stepchild After Changes are Made

Precautions

Mother and stepfather are now together in their own territory. The daughter is situated just a little closer to her mother.

Since the integration of a new relationship with stepchildren is of such great sensitivity, certain precautions are wise.

1. Silence: In the complexity of a family with step-children, silence at times is golden. Never bad-mouth your partner's children. If your partner is letting off steam about a child, listen but do not add fuel to the

fire. You do not even have to agree. For what you say is never forgotten. And even if what you say is true, your comments can come back later to haunt you.

2. The Final Word: Each parent must ultimately make their own decisions as to their children. Unless the decision directly affects the partner or the couple relationship, it is best to take a back seat. If asked, input can be given—but only with the greatest caution.

3. The Past: Don't destroy your new family with a futile attempt to repair the past. Although old loyalties should not be abandoned, the primary loyalty now needs to be to your present partner and your present life.

4. Secret Agendas: Be aware that almost every child of divorce harbors the hope that their parents will get back together. Be understanding of this, but also be on guard to protect your couple relationship from the unconscious, or conscious, wishes of your children and stepchildren.

5. Rules: Rules are often different in different homes. When in your home, a stepchild needs to abide by your rules. Standing together as a couple, and clarifying to the child as to what is expected in your home, can prevent much unnecessary conflict.

The Workshop

STEP #1: Compare The Structural Family Diagrams You Each Have Brought To The Session

What do you see? Are your diagrams different? If so, talk about the differences. Explain to your partner why it is you see things the way you do. No view is the "right" one; each has something to offer. Try to formulate a shared diagram that takes into account both views.

STEP #2: Consideration Of Each Family Member

Look at each family member's circle. First, look at your partner's circle. Is it in proper balance with your circle? Are the circles close enough? Are the lines of communication open between you?

Now, look at each child's circle. Where is it? If it is on the far periphery, can it be brought back into the circle? If it is too close to one parent and too distanced from the other, can the alienated parent make a special effort to reach out and give time to this child—to rebuild confidence, perhaps not love but at least friendship?

Then, look at the members of former families (parents, children, grandparents). How and where are they to be included? Are there problems here that need particular attention? Will one of you, as a former mate, have to put up with more than the other? If so, what can be done to compensate for this?

STEP #3: Identify Structural Problems

How have battle lines been drawn? Are you divided as a couple?

How do the splits occur? Horizontally between generations, or vertically, dividing the family in half? Is one child way out in the cold? Perhaps angry, alone, and alienated? What about the former partners? Are they invading the territory and causing problems?

The goal will be to change your family's structure to that of a healthy family. You will want to realign relationships so that the split is horizontal between generations rather than vertical. You will want to bring the couple, yourselves, together in the central position as leaders of the family. You will want to adjust the power balance so that you, the couple, are in control, not the children.

STEP #4: Identify Power Problems

Is someone, child or adult, wielding too much power? Do some family members have too little power? Do you, as a couple, share a position of equal power?

Power can be defined as the ability to control or influence other family members. Contrary to the myth of the evil stepmother, it is not uncommon for stepchildren to have the greatest power. This is destructive both to the family and to the child. Ideally, power should reside primarily with you, the couple, and that power should be equitably distributed between you.

STEP #5: Clarify Your Roles

Roles differ depending upon the particular family and its situation. No two families are the same. Make sure you, the adults, understand and agree upon your roles.

There are countless variations. For example, in one family, the role of the stepfather may be that of a friend. In another family, the role of the stepfather may be that of a parent. The important thing is that you are both clear about your roles and are in agreement on them.

Discuss with your partner what your role is and what authority you have. Does a particular child try to come between you? If so, how are you going to deal with this?

Try to be comfortable with the role you have. Try not to compete with or criticize the child's biological parent. Step back voluntarily with recognition of the possibly marginal, and yet potentially critical, role you may play in this child's life.

STEP #6: Firm The Boundaries Of Your Couple Relationship

Your first duty is to yourselves and to the creation of a healthy relationship in its own space. You are the leaders. You must take charge. Your needs come first. The vibrations of your relationship set the family tone; stepchildren and non-stepchildren will be impacted by the quality of the waves. Your union as a couple must work if everything is not to fall apart. Your primary obligation is therefore to each other, not to your parents, your former partner, or your children.

Agree to move invaders (children, parents, former mates) to their proper positions. Agree to support each other. Agree to give your partner priority over any other family member. Reaffirm your commitment to each other and to your present family.

STEP #7: Form A Summary Plan

After examining the diagrams you have drawn and discussing the changes you would like to make, agree upon a "plan" that will bring your family into a more desirable balance. This should be brief. It is enough to point in the direction you wish to head. Changes take time. It might be a good idea, once you have decided on the plan, to present it for discussion to the entire family. Explain the lines of authority and control. Get feedback. Be willing to be flexible. Record the plan in your notebooks and agree to evaluate the progress made at the next session.

Chapter 15

Couples And In-Laws

In-laws can be a blessing or a curse. Or they can be both. In-laws are there from the start, hanging on at the periphery. After all, they were you and your partner's families before you created your new family.

In a way, when you become a couple, you sort of leave them behind. You have left their nest and begun your own family. Oh, yes, of course they are still your family. And you love them, and they love you—but all the problems that were there in the past are still there now in the present.

Perhaps some of your in-laws are dominant and intrusive. Perhaps they are rich and powerful. Perhaps they are poor and ill and dependent. Perhaps they are critical, telling you how you should do things. Or perhaps they have gone off into their own lives and couldn't care less about what is happening to you.

We all have all sorts of relatives, and feelings can be very strong. What happens can actually divide you as a couple—tear you apart with loyalties to different family members.

The following workshop, using the principles of Salvador Minuchin's structural family therapy, can be helpful in clarifying the issues as they arise.

The Workshop

Here is a diagram of a healthy family structure that includes in-laws or relatives. After looking at it, draw a picture of your own family's structure, including children and in-laws or other relatives. Place the circles where they are in your family and make their size appropriate to their power.

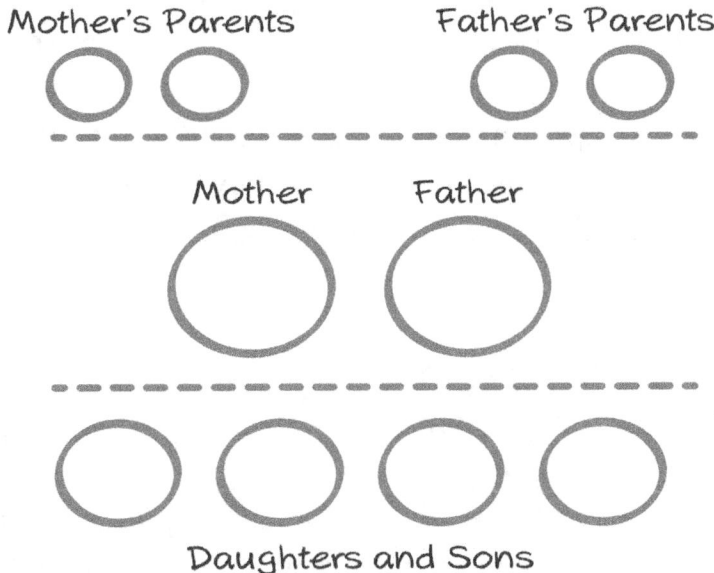

Figure #7: Ideal Family Structure Showing Parents, Children, and In-laws

STEP #1: Each Of You Draw Your Family's Structure

If needed, refer to Chapter 12 for an explanation of Salvador's Minuchin's structural family therapy.

STEP #2: *Compare The Diagrams You Have Made*

Examine the sketches you have each made. Are they similar? Do you agree on placement of the circles and their size?

STEP #3: *Identify The Problems*

Point out to each other the problems you see in the diagrams you have drawn. Are the circles too close? Too distant? Too large? Does the way the circles are placed indicate a problem?

For example, has a father-in-law (loved but feared) been critical of the way your family spends money?

His circle is big and looming over your territory. From the way you have drawn and placed him, you have revealed the problem as well as the action needed. His circle needs to be distanced and made a little smaller.

Has your mother-in-law (loved but oh-so irritating) come for too-long visits?

Her circle is placed next to your partner's in your shared territory. Her circle needs to be taken out of your territory and given a place close but not invading.

Has a sister-in-law (loved but dominating) invaded your lives with demands for attention?

Her circle is shown engulfing your circle within hers. You need to make the circles separate and reduce hers in size. Perhaps you might leave her circle touching your circle, if you like her this close and you both agree.

None of these problems are easy to deal with, but they are part of life. The diagrams you draw can help identify the problems and can be a basis for formulating a plan in which you work together to find a solution.

For example, if a relative becomes ill and needs full-time care, they may want to invade your space, be near you, come and stay with you, have you care for them. You will have to decide, jointly, what path you will follow.

This can be a test of true love. How much can you give up of your personal life? For how long? Under what conditions?

There is no one right answer to these questions. They are questions each couple must resolve for themselves.

STEP #4: Work Together On The Problems You Have Identified And Agree On A Plan Of Action

The solutions you agree upon may depend on which life phase you are in. I know that as part of a young couple I wanted the in-laws to keep their distance.

Now that I'm older and am myself an in-law, my views and wishes are different. I want to move the circles closer and have more frequent visits. I want my circle larger, too. I want to keep my power—after all, even though my children are married and have their own children, to me they are children still!

So, draw the circles, talk together, and decide what needs to change. But remember: although the circles show the ideal for a healthy family, every family has their own "ideal." What you want to determine, and bring about, is the structure that's best for your family, the one bringing love and well-being to each and every family member.

STEP #5: Schedule Another Session To See How Your Plan Is Working

Don't be dismayed if no changes have yet occurred. These are delicate matters, and your plan may need to be altered or, on the other hand, more forcibly exerted. The important thing is that you are aware of the problem, you are working on it, and you are together as a couple.

Epilogue

How sad that couple relationships, so wonderful in the beginning, can so often fall apart with the passage of time. The fact is that most of us are not prepared to be part of a couple. We don't even think of the mechanics of relating; we assume love will carry us through.

Unfortunately, love can be sabotaged by many factors, among which can be such simple things as not knowing how to talk to each other or how to express feelings. Then when major conflicts come up they are difficult to resolve, and smaller conflicts with time can build into major ones.

My goal in writing this book was to help you, as a couple, make the transition from two separate people to two people working together on some of the most important aspects of your relationship: how to communicate, to relate, to compromise, to manage money, to express love and be intimate, and how to handle the complications of children and family.

Today, although these basic principles of relating as a couple have remained the same, in many ways couples are facing a new world.

The role of women has changed, shifting from that of a subsidiary partner to that of an equal partner. Although this change is positive, it presents new and formidable challenges to couples.

The concept of a couples' relationship itself has transformed and broadened to include not only traditionally married couples but also committed couples who choose not to marry and same-sex couples.

And technology has brought new ways of communicating and socializing that have both enhanced and complicated relationships.

Despite all these changes, being part of a couple still remains one of our greatest joys. We have a companion through the difficulties of life, a sexual partner, someone who makes us "special" and whom we make "special."

I hope the workshops have helped strengthen your relationship as a couple, and that as new issues arise you will add chapters and workshops of your own.

Remember, though, that the workshops cannot solve all problems. They are certainly worth a try, but if emotions are too strong, or the problems too complex (infidelity, drug addiction, severe financial problems, etc.), professional help will be needed.

I know such help is not always available, for financial or other reasons; however, if it is, I urge you to take advantage of it. Sometimes people hold back because of the stigma of "having to have therapy," but don't let false pride interfere—too much is at stake!

And sometimes even professional help is not enough. If, after all your efforts, your relationship ends, have hope. You are not alone.

Take what you have learned from the relationship. Try to salvage the positive and let the negative go. As bleak as things may seem, and as painful as the loss is, life is full of twists and turns, and the future lies ahead unknown. If you are open to a new relationship, chances are it will come your way.

And for those of you who have had success using the book—who have become better able to communicate, to compromise and resolve problems, to be intimate, and to express love openly—

CONGRATULATIONS!

You have come a long way toward creating a better relationship—now you are not only partners in love but partners in life as well.

www.ingramcontent.com/pod-product-compliance
Lightning Source LLC
Chambersburg PA
CBHW060253290526
45789CB00001B/307